THIRTY BLACKS IN BRITISH EDUCATION
HOPES, FRUSTRATIONS, ACHIEVEMENTS

Don Henry
edited by Ralph Ruddock

RABBIT
PRESS

First published January 1991

Published by RABBIT PRESS LIMITED
18 Batemans Court, Crawley, Sussex RH10 6PS, England

ISBN O 948775 03 3

Copyright: University of Manchester

Printed in Great Britain by Biddles of Guildford

PREFACE

DONALD PETER HENRY was born in Trinidad in 1935. He was one of eight children in a rather poor family. He received only a rudimentary education for no money was available to maintain him at a secondary school. In his early twenties he moved to England where he worked as a storeman with a television rental company in London. He knew of no way towards entry into the education he had always desired; the chance perusal of a poster on a wall in Mornington Crescent led him to evening classes - three a week - for 'O' levels and later for 'A' levels. He was accepted for a social science degree course in the Manchester Polytechnic and received a grant. After graduation, he qualified at the Bolton College for Technical Teachers in 1969 and in 1970 was appointed Lecturer at the South Trafford College.

He followed this with an M.Ed. in Manchester University in 1975-1976, for which he was grant-aided. He was accepted for doctoral-level part-time research on the experience of Blacks in the British education system. After six years of work, he was awarded the degree of Ph.D. in 1986. This book is extracted from his thesis, in which he recorded some of his own experiences under the name of Peter (case history No. 30).

Don Henry was a man of great warmth and astonishing energy. He was active in a wide and varying range of networks, notably including the students' union in the large college in which he taught. The students' response to him was very positive, and still is, in the form of donations from their social functions to the research fund which has been set up in his memory. He was also known for his work in the field of housing, and among the West Indian communities of Greater Manchester. Beyond this, he kept himself fit, and played a vigorous game of football on Saturdays.

It is against this background, together with a heavy teaching commitment, that one marvels to record his seven years of part-time research to meet the requirements for the degree of Ph.D. How demanding this is can only be appreciated by those who have tried it. For this academic work, his employing authority did not grant any remission of his teaching, nor did he receive any financial help whatever.

Don was married to a Scottish school teacher. There were two children, a boy and a girl, both presently making good progress in graduate-level technical education.

Don was a grand example of all that is good in Caribbean culture: warm, sociable and full of life. He died of a cancer of the liver, when his life was reaching a new level of attainment. His death left all who knew him with feelings of bitter grief. His real concern for other people revealed his religious orientation. He did not speak much about this, but in his final weakness he found the solace and strength he had always sought through prayer and faith. He died in February, 1988 and was buried in Manchester. 'So he passed over, and all the trumpets sounded for him on the other side'.

INTRODUCTION

THE CASE HISTORIES which form the bulk of this book report the experiences of respondents whose ages ranged from the teens to the eighties. They were gathered between 1983 and 1986. All were of African descent, except for the White wife of one subject. Their educational experiences in Britain included some as early as the 1920's, others from later decades, and a few who had recently left school. Most had engaged in some form of post-school training or learning. It is possible to note some changes of attitude, school practice and race relations over the period of seventy years, as reported; and some respects in which there has not been much change.

As Don Henry wrote, the book is to be read as a contribution to oral history, presenting verbatim accounts as recorded. It is not a social-scientific exercise in measurement, nor an attempt to develop theory. Many of the interviews were lengthy, so a rigorous selection was made from the great abundance of very rich material. This was done by focussing on themes considered to be primarily of interest to educationists and teachers, but also to all, Black or White, who have themselves passed through

the British school or post-school systems. Much of the
background biographical data reported by the subjects, as
well as their own thoughts and perceptions, had to be
omitted, though a considerable amount will be found in
their statements.

All of these histories bear the hallmark of genuine,
even impassioned, expression. The dramas of involvement
and alientation; of endeavour and failure; of resolute
engagement with all the tasks and difficulties and, in a
number of cases, achievement and recognition after years
of rejection or indifference, will be found on every page.
And let us remember those whose school experience turned
them against learning, apparently for life. That also is
a drama.

Don Henry has listed his own selection of 'salient
points' all of real substance. As one who can claim many
years of involvement with Don and his work, as personal
friend and research supervisor and now, as his editor, I
would stress a few outcomes of his work which he did not
have the chance to develop before his untimely death.

First, anyone who reads these personal stories must
be impressed by the prevailing naive hopefulness which
characterised the entry of these Black citizens, young or
adult, into their education in this country. In many
cases,they had arrived with idealised images of England,
propogated in their Caribbean or West African homelands.
They expected things to be good. What they found was not
good: in some instances, it was so bad they could hardly
believe it. It was true, also, perhaps excepting very
recent years, that those born in Britain approached their
school education with real hopes, which often stemmed from
their parents, who saw education as the road to an
improvement of their condition. At least they expected a
fair chance in the education system, and support from
their teachers. They expected to be taught and to be
given learning tasks. They would have welcomed stricter
teachers, and they responded to those who were demanding.
In almost every case, there was progressive
disenchantment; and, later, a gradual realisation of the
weight of a system that 'selected them out'.

How could their parents have understood that their
local schools were likely to be among the worst, in any
city? Or that the teachers in such schools often saw
themselves as failures because they did not succeed in

finding posts in 'better schools': that such teachers, and often head teachers, were utterly demoralised in the face of what they saw as a hopeless task? And, in addition, that White children often react with equal disappointment and progressive disillusion?

Our own experience - with White children -has sometimes been as follows: School X is generally thought to be a bad school. Unpublished researches bear out this reputation: the school is found to have high levels of delinquency, truancy, and of pregnancy; and of staff turnover. H.M.I. have repeatedly reported unfavourably on it (but their reports at that time were not made available). Parents generally know that the school has a poor reputation but do not know what rights they may have in entering their children into another school. They do not have a firm basis for choice, as it is the policy of the Authority not to publish school indices, or even rates of success in examinations and statistics of entrants to further or higher education. There is some awareness that, in Britain, the head has an almost absolute authority and, therefore, responsibility to determine whatever issues arise in the daily life of his or her school; so the head's views are sought. The likely comments : 'This is a bad school. Everyone knows that it is a bad school. I knew it before I took on the headship; but what can I do? The staff are disaffected: they are all trying to move elsewhere. The parents are apathetic and the youngsters hostile. How am I to change all that?' Perhaps the head feels that morale in British urban schools will come to approximate that in New York or Los Angeles, with truancy rates over fifty percent, drugs and hand-guns traded amongst pupils, teachers assaulted, raped even murdered.

Sociologists have highlighted the pathology of poor schools in deprived urban areas. They have helped us to understand how such a school comes to be what it is. If, however, 'the point is to change it', they have less to offer.

How can one expect the Black parents to know, even approximately, what they are putting their children into when they start school? Don Henry rightly rejects the notion that families within Black cultures are inherently defective. Virtually all the Black parents in his study emerge as 'caring'to a greater or lesser degree.

Most of the early Black immigrants were men, and many married White women. The role of these women as wives and mothers to a Black family in a White society was crucial. They understood better the British social system within which they had grown up, and often took issue with the school if at some point it was evident that their child was unfairly treated. Even so, their knowledge was necessarily limited, as is that of all parents in respect of the school system. Much poor teaching or bad treatment was endured, because parents did not know their rights, or did not understand the reasons for decisions made about their children. It is an act of courage for a parent to enter a school and attempt to argue a case on the basis of scant knowledge.

Knowledge of the system, and especially of post-school opportunities for work and adult learning, is perhaps the single most stressed item in these life histories. Their lack of knowledge, and the lack of any agency to help them to know, was keenly felt by most of the respondents. There were many false starts, many delays, much time wasted in non-relevant studies; all for lack of a guidance and counselling system. This was as true for those aspiring to higher education as for those who dropped out at the school level. Don Henry wondered what his own history might have been if he had not chanced to see a notice saying 'Working Men's College', in Mornington Crescent; after which, he had 'no idea how to move into higher education... so had to go about blindly searching'.

This is clearly an issue of great significance. Information systems under designated officers, since that time, have been set up in all local education authorities; but we need to know how effective their penetration is, and how complete their coverage. It was not many years ago that in a large conurbation like Manchester, there was nobody who could advise an enquirer whether a specialist course he or she was seeking was an offer in Oldham, Bury, Altrincham, or Stockport - all within a bus ride - if not in Manchester itself. Certainly, the mass of information required for reference is enormous; but every travel bureau demonstrates the technology of instant video display of data from a central source. How else are we to eliminate those pathetic instances of waste where a person devotes two years or more of rigorous evening study to qualify for a course that, in the event, no longer requires that kind of preparation. Training for social work has been a case in point. Such waste still occurs: on what scale, no-one knows.

Lack of knowledge, lack of help towards knowledge, was a significant factor in the heartfelt bitterness that pervades these personal accounts. Most of this derives from the almost daily experience of racial discrimination, often in the faceless institutional firms where less qualified White people are seen to be chosen for paid work, for promotion, or for further training; or, still more often, in the form of open or veiled insult. Both forms of racism are reported to be manifest within British education. However, in some forms of high education, a total absence of such discrimination was noted, and much appreciated.

The police, on the other hand, are uniformly reported as hostile and viciously abusive to all Blacks. Their behaviour, apparently, regularly takes the form of totally illegal physical abuse and harassment of all young Blacks, regardless of any grounds for suspicion. It is certain that very many entirely innocent young Blacks are physically intimidated and assaulted by the police, as a routine practice. It would seem that police strategy is to require Black people to be invisible, perhaps confined in a ghetto or, better still, to persecute them to the point where they will seek to emigrate. No regard is paid to the consideration that young Black people are full citizens and British born.

All respondents seem to agree that, whereas the earlier Black immigrants accepted discrimination and insult without protest, the younger generation certainly will not do so. There is ample evidence that this accords with change of self-image, a gradual process that is manifest decade by decade. As in the United States, contemptuous White attitudes were internalised within the Black cultures, often to the point of some degree of self-contempt. The improvement in self-image is crucial for educational performance. There is ample evidence for educational psychologists that a capacity for learning partly depends on confidence that one can learn. There is no more significant finding for assimilation and practice on the part of all teachers of Black children.

It will be noted that a number of the. respondents were raised in Catholic childrens homes, foster families

and Catholic schools. Many have been savagely critical of
the treatment they received.   Some have been bitterly
resentful of the attitude of the nuns towards them, which
for some was enough to turn them against their church
permanently.   Don Henry transcribed their statements from
the tape, exactly as they came to him.   He was himself a
Catholic and loyal on the whole, although with some long
periods of detachment.   There can be no doubt that the
Roman Catholic Church had, or did have, a deficiency in
the selection and training of sisters charged with the
responsibilities for children, especially Black children.

I would like to register my impression - which I am
certain will be echoed by all readers of these histories -
of the remarkable qualities of character shown by almost
all of these respondents.   Their persistence, and their
achievements, in the fact of so many difficulties, leaves
one feeling chastened, to say the least.   As these
qualities were so abundantly evident in my late friend, I
am happy to end on that positive note.

Ralph Ruddock
Manchester   July 1989

Don Henry dedicated his researches to his parents, for whom he had a deep affection, as he had for all his friends and relatives in Trinidad. He expressed his warm gratitude to his respondents; and he wished to name the following for their generous help:

ROBERT ARMSTRONG
STEVE EDGELL
JO FREEMAN
PATRICIA HURST
NUR HUSSEIN
CATHRYN LANYON
EILISH McAULEY
TERESA O'BRIEN
RALPH RUDDOCK
PAULINE SIMM
RACHEL SMITH
JOHN STOCKTING

He also named the Afro-Caribbean community in Manchester, whose kinship he so much valued; and Kate Evans, who gave him the greatest support, especially in his last years.

IT HAS BEEN thought useful to present first the personal story of Ms. X. This will, it is hoped, serve more than one purpose, the principal one being to acquaint the reader with the richness of content, the style of recording, the authenticity and impact of the case histories to follow.

CASE HISTORY 1 : MS.X.

I **WAS BORN** in the U.K. and fostered at an early age. I have never met my parents, though I believe my mother was a nurse of Irish background. The foster agency I went to was run by Catholic nuns and they made a lasting impression on me.

My first memory of school was at the age of six which coincided with my first semi-permanent fostering to a White family. Before this I remember vaguely many foster homes, but not school days. Both my foster parents were White, and I was one of nine other children in this home, five White and four Black. Later on more Black children were fostered. At school I experienced racial taunts especially about my hair; even the teachers made such comments and then complained about my attitude to them. Also because my real mum was Irish my foster parents sent me to Irish dancing. I hated it, and this caused lots of problems. It was at that time I first knew that I could be silent. One day my foster mum called me a liar when I answered to a question she asked. I went straight up to my room and stayed there, not talking to anybody. I was also supposed to go to Irish dancing and refused to. The next thing I knew was that the agency which fostered me came and took me away. While I was back at the fostering agency I shared a bedroom with this girl who called me names and this ended in a fight. It was the first time I rebelled against people calling me Black. I was aware that I was different and not White, but I did not associate at this stage with being Black, as my whole life was with White people. Some weeks later I was taken to another foster home. There were other Black children there and that made me feel better.

It took me some time to come to terms with my new parents, and about a year before I called them mum and dad. I just closed off from everybody. I went to the local primary school and in an art lesson we were drawing and painting hands. The teacher was mixing paint colours to match our hands. She asked us all to put our hands on the table. We did, and she said to me that I needed a pinky colour. I just sat there and looked at my hands, then looked at everybody else's and thought, mine aren't pink? I did not say anything and just followed the rest of the class, because I thought I did not want it to be any different for me. I was new to the class anyway. I remember changing to junior school and being loud and disruptive. My work did not suffer but my school reports at that time showed that I was moved around the class to stop me talking. It was at about this time I became aware of what fostering was. My foster brother who was White was in the same junior class as me but was treated differently. Everything I did or said I was told off for. My foster brother was adopted and I was not. One day on our way to school I asked him why can't his surname be like mine? We live in the same house. Why was mine to be different? How come the kids ask me why you are White and I am not? It was that sort of thing I had to come to terms with while at junior school.

When I asked my parents about adoption and fostering, they would always say that it is a long story and that I will be told when I was older. The question was always by-passed even when we went into junior three. There I was put in a separate class from my foster brother in what was the year before eleven plus. In the first term I worked hard and was conscious that the people in my class was very different from his. Most of the people in the eleven plus class lived in the posh area and those in my

class mainly came from council estates. My best friend
lived on one of the council estates and I used to go to
her house. I was unaware that I was not to invite her to
my house, because it was in the posh part. I was told by
my foster mom to stay away from people who lived in those
areas as they were not very nice people. I used to ask
why because I liked my friend, but I never got any other
answer.

I got good results in that class and after Christmas
I was put in the 'A' class of junior three which was the
same as my foster brother's. However, it was not until
junior four that things started to fit into place. I did
not really like junior four as I made all my friends in
the other class and my old friends called me 'snobby', and
refused to walk home with me. I wanted to go back to the
class I was in but was told I could not.

In junior four we started getting lots of homework
and assessment papers and my marks was always low. Every
Friday we had mock exams and I just could not be bothered.
I could not care less even though I was not aware of the
real importance of the test. What brought it home to me
was that three other girls who the teacher preferred were
talking about the exams, what their parents were going to
give them, and where they will go when they passed. The
girls' families were well known in the Parish, and with it
being a Catholic school all the parents used to talk to
each other. I could not figure out then why the girls did
not want to talk to me. I however saw the high marks the
girls were getting and realised how low mine was. I then
felt I wanted to beat them, I am going to beat them.
During this time my parents was helping my foster brother
a lot and I was 'shutting off'. They did not offer any
help and I did not ask for any. To be honest, I just did
not know how to ask for it. By then I had realised the
importance of the eleven plus and why everyone was
panicking. I started going home and spending hours in my
room doing my homework. Like the others I would hand in
my homework and each Monday the teacher would read out the
marks. This particular week I came top. I had beaten my
foster brother and the three girls. I got 98%. The
teacher asked me who helped me. I said nobody and that
was the truth. When I got home I told my parents my
results, they also asked me who helped me. I told them
no-one, as they knew that I was in my room by myself. It

was then they said if I needed any help they will give it
to me. My attitude was, if they could not offer before I
don't need it now. I knew they treated my foster brother
as their son and that I was not on the same level. I look
back now and realise that I was not the only one, the
other children in the house were also aware of it. It may
be hard to say now but looking back, they fostered me for
financial reasons. I've thought of it many times and I am
positive that this was their reason. I therefore tried to
relate more closely to the school. My maths was my weak
subject and I asked my teacher if I could stay behind and
do extra maths, he said yes; and this helped to get me
through the eleven plus. My other incentive to pass the
eleven plus was that I would get a bike and I wanted one as
the others had bikes. On passing I went to Technical High
School and my brother went to Grammar. Because of this he
was seen as more successful than me. I had no opportunity
to go to the Catholic Girls Grammar but when I went there
for the entrance exams and found it was nuns who run it I
did not want to go.

    The fostering agency was run by nuns and I hated
them, they frightened me. All I could remember nuns for
was telling me off or hitting me. There was no sort of
warmth coming from them, and every time I was fostered it
was the nuns who drove me somewhere and left me. They
never attempted to explain anything to me. During the
entrance exam, which was easy, I did not try. I just sat
there waiting for the time so I could go home. I went to
technical school instead. At technical school I was aware
that my teachers knew I was fostered and that was why they
treated me different. I knew that I was rowdy and naughty
and was always being sent out from the class. The reason
for my behaviour at that time was that I was looking for
security.   I also realised that being competitive and
winning meant that I got lots of attention, so I got
pretty good at that. I remember a teacher in junior four
asking the class, which one of us wanted a new wallet. I
looked around the class and everybody wanted it and I
could not understand why. I then thought I'll see if I
can get it, and I did. This particular teacher was well
liked as he used to take special students to the theatre
to see Gilbert and Sullivan and such.

    At the technical school, the teachers used to palm us
off by saying this school (technical) was like the

grammar, with a wider range of subjects to choose from. My other early memory of technical school was that there was another Black girl in the same class as me. I identified with her very strongly and even wanted my hair combed like hers. This girl was a trouble maker, though she did not react when the other kids called her about her colour and her features. I was the opposite, I could not stand people calling me. I can't have people laughing at me because I am not the same as them. So I decided not to sit next to her because she gave in. She even carried their books which I would never do. She was also the one they set up for pranks and because I removed myself from all of them they called me creep.

In my first year at technical school I came last in class and was frightened to take my report home. I did not get in trouble and all my foster dad said was 'you're not doing too well are you?' I said no, and he signed it. It is at this stage I realised that I had closed my foster parents out of my school life. They did not know what was going on at school until there was. some trouble in the second year.

In that year I enjoyed religious studies until we got this nun as our teacher. I hated both her and the subject. She was always picking on me and the other Black girl. The White girls used to tell us that she did not like us Blacks. I told them I knew that and I was not bothered. I was games captain at that time, and happy. One day my socks kept falling, the nun told me to put them back up and when I did they fell again. In front of the whole class she told me off. I felt really embarrassed. She then told me to take my socks off and walk around the class room ten times. I refused. She took my captain's badge off me. I took my bag and walked out. The nun threatened to remove me from the netball team and I told her she could do what she liked. Later I found out that all the girls in the class supported me, because they knew I really loved netball and that I was not in the wrong. I went home really upset and told my mum what had happened. Parents Evening was near and my mum said she would take up the matter then. I thought it would be awkward for my mum as I did not know how much of me the nun knew. My mum was White you see! However my mum took the word of the nun against mine. She always took the word of teachers anyway, I should've known. In front of me the nun denied my story and said I dropped my games captain's badge outside the classroom. I refused to take the badge back or to apologise as I knew that I was in the right. I later saw the girls in the class and told them at the next religious class, no one was to answer questions or do any work. They all agreed saying that she did treat me horribly. The nun realised what was happening and naturally blamed me, but her attitude towards me changed a bit as she knew I could get the class to boycott her lessons.

In my second year I had this geography teacher who was really nasty to me. We had a dismerits system for not wearing uniform properly, walking down the wrong side of the corridor and so on. The prefects were the ones who used to give them out but the geography teacher told my prefect to watch me. I got on with my work despite the situation and out of ten subjects in the second year I came first in seven, and fourth overall. I got poor marks in religious studies and geography. I did very well in biology. In fact my favourite teacher was the biology/P.E. teacher. I really admired her. She did not try to stop me being independent or single minded, and she was the first person I felt any warmth from. She actually cared not just for schooling, but for me as an individual person. At this time in my life, I still did not see treatment to me in strict black and white terms. A lot of the awful response to me I thought, was because I was fostered. I was also very embarrassed to take friends home because of this. I remember telling one girl of my situation, and it was the only time I told anyone away from home. This girl turned around and said, you are a bastard then? Obviously I had heard people using that word before in a spiteful manner, but I did not know what it meant until I looked it up in my dictionary. That was when I realised what it was all about and why I was at the agency. My life fitted together.

I then started to mix with another Black girl older than myself, and she told me about Angela Davis and the Black Power movement. I was third year, she was fifth. We never mixed at school, so the authorities did not know that we took the same bus to and from school and talked about not being White. In talking I realised, that many incidents that happened to her happened to me as well. I then remembered telling my foster sister, who was of West

Indian parentage, black sambo - a name the kids at school used to call me - I felt really horrible and said to myself what am I calling her for. The whole thing made me realise that I was Black as well. In the fourth year I felt and became aware of racism as a young Black woman. While in the third year, we had to choose our 'O' level options, and I deliberately chose biology as I wanted to do nursing. I liked Chemistry and I liked Needlework so I chose them with options French and German, also Economics as it was a new subject. In the fourth year we got a new headmistress. At about this time my best friend - a White girl - was going out with this Black lad, and she took him to the school discos. The new headmistress found out and rang the girl's mum telling her about her daughter's boyfriend. The parents were really angry, and the girl told the headmistress that it was none of her business. I supported her and we were both sent home. My 'O' level preparations deteriorated and instead of nine 'O' levels I ended up doing three and three C.S.E's. I failed miserably, getting one 'O' level grade B, two C.S.E. grades 1 and R.S.A. stage 1. The Black girl whom I spoke of earlier went to live in London with her parents, as a result my best friend was now a Chinese girl. She was born in this country and we realised we had lots in common, as she also got hassles about her race. We went everywhere together and a very close friendship developed between us. During school holidays we both got part-time jobs in the same place. It was while doing this part-time job I realised that I could win people over if I used my personality. This Saturday job coincided with my declining 'O' level preparation. There was also a lack of motivation on my part and no encouragement from home. I was also comparing myself with my foster sister who went to Grammar School and was given less housework to do. In defending her my parents used to say that I will not need my 'O' levels as I will be married in a few years time. Unlike me my foster sister was well behaved. She was also bright, but I knew that I was as bright as her.

On the whole I enjoyed school betwen the end of my fourth year and all of the fifth year. We had great relationships with the teachers, that is until the careers sessions. The teachers tried to palm us off with all sorts of jobs. Everything they chose for me I turned down. I now wanted to learn some more, not go out to work. Also, I was getting no advice from home. One day I picked up a brochure which told me that I could continue my education while training. That I could participate in sporting events and get a salary on top of that. At that time there was one Black policewoman in our area, whom I knew and who supported my joining the force. I had heard negative stuff about the police but did not pay much attention to it. The teachers said they were happy with my choice as it was a secure job, but they did not actually help in my choice of career.

Joining the force meant that I lived away from home, as a result my relationship with my foster parents hardened. During my first year in the force I struck up a permanent relationship with a White lad; he was not a cadet. Our relationship ended as his mother rejected me because I was Black, and he gave in to his mother. I also found that the male cadets I went out with socially became nasty because I refused to get involved with them. My non-compliance was put down to the fact that I was strange because I was Black. At this stage, they started calling me coon, wog and nigger. The cadet girls also got at me. The reason for their behaviour was that I was doing well and was offered a driving course as a result. Getting on the driving course was like getting gold, and I was told the girls felt I was getting it because I was Black. I reported both incidents to the superintendent. In advising me to put up with it, he said that being Black is like having eczema and that anything which is not right in this society will get knocked. That Black people aren't seen as right yet. He however advised me against leaving. I stayed only because they gave me an opportunity to get my 'O' levels at the local tech.

It was at tech I found strength in my identity. There were many more Black people there and for the first time I got on great with all my lecturers. It was also an opportunity to do subjects I had never done before. This period was the best I've had in education. I was really motivated and my marks reflected this. I did five 'O' levels, including Politics and Sociology, and got two A's, two B's and a C. The lecturers suggested I did A levels, and hinted at the possibility of my going to university or polytechnic. At this time things were still not right with my foster parents and me and we parted company. Putting things together in my head I realised that it was

not only racism but also the inability to cope with being
fostered which influenced my situation. I continued to
question many things about my life and the lecturers at
college supported this way of thinking. The racial
harassment I was getting in the force made my decision
easy. I then packed the police in on the pretence that I
wanted to try something else. The lad who rejected me was
at Teacher Training College and I remembered talking to him
him about work at the college. I then felt that I could
do as well, or even better, so I applied while doing my
'A' levels. I got into teacher training and thought it
was the end of the struggle, but it was not. My foster
dad for some reason contacted me and became very
supportive. He took me aside and told me I was doing the
right thing as success in education was the only way for
Black people to get on. He also said he realised the
hassles I've been through but I must not give in. He gave
me more support than my foster mother.

At the teacher training college I experienced racism
from the girls in halls. I was the only Black girl in the
first year and they resented my friendship with this White
guy. A number of students were also surprised that a
Black person, especially a Black girl, could get good 'A'
levels and make it to college. Some of them actually
asked me if I really got my 'A' levels. On my first
teaching practice, during my first year at college, I was
posted to this local school with many Black and Asian
kids. When I got to the staff room I introduced myself
and the member of staff with whom I was going to work,
said in front of all the other staff, 'I did not realise
that the student teacher was Black, they did not tell me'.
I felt awful. She then said to me 'Are you full-breed or
half-breed?' I was shattered and thought, God! you get
this everywhere you turn, even from educated people. At
the training college I found that I could talk to my
tutor, he always listened and was a good counsel. He and
fellow students told me to be careful, not to be over
sensitive as I could ruin my teaching practice. I was
expected to ignore this in a school where there was a high
percentage of Black children. I then did what I always do
when I get this kind of pressure. I shut myself off from
everybody. My course tutor later promised to move me if I
wanted but I stuck it out and got good marks for my
teaching practice.

The college also provided me with an opportunity for sports, especially track and field events. I got on very well with the head of P.E., maybe it's because I was older and well motivated. By this stage, I was becoming an international athlete with a chance of going to the Commonwealth Games. The college was very helpful and positive towards my intentions in athletics. It was the first time the system was actually used to help me. I was also told by the Principal that when I got a job in teaching I will meet up with lots of hostility, and may even have to work in a Black country. He told me not to give up as I had a lot to offer.

I realised at that stage in my life that schooling did nothing for me nor for the friends that I had known, especially the Black friends. We all got our qualifications and satisfaction after leaving school. In further education we saw the value of education, which was more than just learning for an 'O' level. The teachers were dedicated and seemed to enjoy teaching. They listened to us and were prepared to give up their spare time to help us. I was really influenced by that attitude. The teacher training college was fantastic with regards career advice, they kept me fully informed with posts that were going. Also, for the first time I felt mentally free of fostering, racism and sexism, even though it existed around me. I felt I knew where I was going. During this time I made the international scene in athletics and was accepted for my ability and as a person. I was well ranked and represented Great Britain in many meetings overseas. I was getting invitations left, right and centre and was overwhelmed. I have never had success like this before and I realised that to handle it I had to be detached, ruthless and competitive. I did not find that hard to do.

Having completed my teaching certificate course I wrote off for jobs and had a number of interviews. On some of these interviews they actually said to me 'You did not tell us you were Black'. I never said it but I used to think, why should I have to tell them that, I am a fully qualified teacher. Incidentally, I had a Black friend at college whose policy was to stick a photograph on every application form he sent off. I refused to do that. In an interview in Handsworth, Birmingham, the headmaster, though at first non-committal about my getting the post, suggested to me that I could start looking for places to live in Birmingham. As a result of that hint I thought I had got the job. Four weeks later I still had not heard from him, and during that time I had stopped applying for other posts. I rang the school and was told that the post was already filled. I asked why I did not get it and was told that it was because I could not teach maths. I said the post advertised was for P.E. and Science, which I am qualified for and the question of maths teaching never came up in the interview. The headmaster said he was terribly sorry but that I did not get the job. I was devastated, as everything seemed right and the school had a large Black population. I did think at the time 'I will be alright here'. I was advised by the college not to take the matter further as it would be difficult to prove bias, and that sort of action may go against me when applying for other jobs. I reluctantly accepted the college's advice.

August came and I did not have a job. I was getting worried. I applied for supply teaching and got a post in an almost all-White school. The fourth and fifth years gave me a hard time, a lot of racial harassment. I tried to be reasonable and very often ended up crying. I went to the head about it. He felt I ought to be more authoritarian with them and that I was taking things too personal. While there I noticed how other teachers behaved. What stood out was the dislike many teachers had for the kids they taught. Some sent the kids out of the classroom and said how much they hated them. That brought everything about my school years back to me. I thought, how the hell can they expect the kids to learn or to appreciate the importance of a constructive relationship. I did not actually say anything but I got into a lot of trouble for not toeing the line. I refused to relate to the kids like them. One of the teachers told me that she thought I was arrogant and aggressive. I did not bother with her. I felt I had some success with the kids. While there, I took over running the netball team and we won the schools championship for the first time. I did this without being authoritarian, but that did not satisfy some staff. While on supply I applied for and got another post teaching Biology and P.E. At that interview the head told me that I would be the only Black teacher in the school. He asked me how do I think I would cope with that, did I think it would bother me? I said that I would be able to cope, it won't bother me, though it may some staff and students. It will be a learning situation for all of us. He said he liked that response and I got the job. I taught there for three years.

This was my first experience of teaching many Black children. There were three of them in my first class. I noticed that they were very distant and cautious of me. One of the girls was very good at sport and I felt that to be a meeting point. She reminded me of myself, years back. The other girl was adopted and this was an issue that helped in our relationship. She talked if there was no one else around and I felt I was able to help her and the class understand her situation. This was a good class. They listened and participated. One White kid said to me that he would not like to be called names, like they called Jenny (the Black girl) as that was not nice, not fair and it must hurt. I began to realise then that it is possible to get through to some White kids this thing about racism. It was another learning situation for me.

Other classes presented a problem, there were kids who would not come into my class because I was not White, and they said so. This was happening during the riots in 1981. The kids in the upper school were given National Front literature at the school gates, and as far as I knew the headmaster did nothing about it. They wrote on the board in my classroom 'Wogs Out', 'Niggers Out', and 'Miss X is a wog'. I refused to ignore this as I thought of the Black children involved. I went to the head, told him, and gave him an exercise book with similar statements in it. The head said that he could do nothing about the statements but he could reprimand the lad for defacing school property. I just looked at him and thought; I don't believe this. I refused to have this child in my class. The following day the deputy head said to me I should not blame the child because anybody with a disability will be seen as different. I asked her if she meant being Black was being disabled. She said yes.

It was not unusual to hear racist remarks in the staffroom. I have been told by a colleague to get back where I came from. They asked me about West Indian foods and what it was like to live in one of those ghetto areas? I pulled one teacher up for a racist remark she made and

she told me she meant other Blacks as I was O.K.   I
received no support from the head nor staff, other than
two young teachers.   I was even advised by the deputy head
that it would be better if I taught in a school with many
Blacks, with people of my own type, as I will never be
accepted in this society.   She mentioned the effect that
fostering had on me -information that I was surprised she
had - and suggested I spent more time with people I could
identify with.   I couldn't believe it, I was so hurt.   I
gave in and put in for a transfer which I got.   I spent
one term in yet another school between transfer.   Both
these schools had a higher Black population.   I am still
at this second school.   I felt before joining this school
that staff will be more racially aware and, on the whole,
most of them are.   The headmaster is trying with a liberal
approach, though one particular member of staff is on
record as saying I could not fit into White culture.   He
also stated that together Blacks look threatening.
'You've got to watch them'.

The education system has been useful to me in shaping
my attitude.   What I got was not because of, but despite,
the system.   The schooling system does not set out to help
Black people succeed.   I only realised my potential in
further and higher education, and even there problems
exist.   At teaching college I was asked to stay on for the
fourth year for my degree, but had to refuse due to my
financial situation.   I hope with my qualifications and
experience I could get on to the diploma course at the
local university.   I have applied for secondment, but if I
don't get that I will try part-time.   I am particularly
interested in Womens Studies,which is not part of schools
education.   Though it ought to be.   I want to be involved
in the education of Black people.   I came to realise race
mainly through Black music in early adolescence.   However,
being aware of race is not the same as being conscious of
the depth of racism in the society.   That consciousness
came out of personal relationships and realising that
educated people, teachers, could be very racist.   There are
many Black teachers who share similar experiences.   Some
are not fighting it just in case it affects their career
and promotion prospects.   My foster sister got a place at
university but did not accept it, she was looking for a
job.   I have not seen my foster parents for years and have
no inclination to contact them.   If given the opportunity I
would like to meet my Dad.

Ms. X's education, especially up to secondary, was heavily influenced by her experience of being fostered, and her relations with nuns.

Ms. X rejected a possible grammar school place because of the presence of nuns in the institution.

Ms. X notes the willingness of parents to accept the teachers views.

Teacher training raised her awareness in the areas of politics and schooling. A good careers service existed and the programme was designed to help respective teachers in every way.

Ms. X somewhat astonished to find racism among teaching staff in schools.

A knowledge of the existence of racial groups and of racial consciousness not always related, according to Ms. X.

Significant aspects of Ms. X's learning took place outside the organisation of the school.

CASE HISTORY 2 : ERNEST MARKE

Born in Freetown, Sierra Leone.   Settled in England in
1917, at the age of fourteen.   A retired seaman and
author, his autobiographical work 'Ole Man Trouble' was
published by Heinemann.   Mr   Marke is married with five
children.

ON ARRIVAL IN Liverpool, I went to live with the
ship's steward and his family in Wavertree.   One of his
three children was my age and I went to the same school as
them.   I left when I was fifteen years of age, but I
remember that while I was at that school I was very
frustrated because I was the subject of curious, racist
reactions, and I did not like it.   This behaviour was from
both children and teachers.   In fact, they were all
surprised that I could read and write.   'How did you
learn, where did you learn?', they asked.   I remember the
teacher giving me a test and she too was surprised of my

ability to understand the work, she said that there was no education in Africa. All these things got me frustrated. The reason why I ran away from school in Africa, and stowed away to England, was not because I did not want education, but I always wanted adventure, I wanted to see the world.

I was also surprised by the reaction of the people to me when I went to church with the family. The congregation obviously did not want me there. On leaving school I got a job on board a merchant ship as a cabin boy, a job I did before on the journey from Africa to England. I thought this was the best way to learn, especially after my experience of school in Wavertree.

When I came back to Liverpool after months at sea, I left the ship to get a job on land. I found it very difficult to get a job, in fact all Black people found it difficult to get work as the soldiers were coming back home from the war, and they were given preference. Where the Black man had a job he was sacked so that the White man could get that job. Blacks could not get jobs even to sweep the streets of England. This situation of unemployment and the racist reaction by the Whites to the Black man was the main reason behind the race riots of 1919 in Liverpool, Cardiff, and even Glasgow. Because of this, Black people were offered free passages (repatriation) to Africa or the West Indies. The Government offered £6 for each Black person taking up the offer. £1 to be given on embarkation, and £5 on arrival at the destination. Many Blacks, most of them seamen, tried to get work on ships, but where this was possible, Black seamen got £6 and White seamen got £9.10s. The Elder Dempster Line was the main shipping line employing Blacks, and at this time Blacks tried to unionise, but Elder Dempster would not have it, they sacked the lot of us Blacks. White men were allowed to unionise and they took our jobs as stokers, though in those days stoking was a Black man's job. Naturally, the Black men forgot unions and accepted the £6. Not many of us Blacks got jobs with Elder Dempster and I was one of the very few who accepted repatriation. I went to what was then called British Guiana, as there was talk of gold to be found there. This whole adventure was not successful and I slipped back into England. Unemployment for the Black person was still high and though I have always considered continuing my education formally, it took all my strength and guile to raise enough money to pay my rent, and at that time there were no groups or organisations to give guidance to the Black man on such matters. At that time the Blacks who were in education were either the children of mixed marriages in schools, and the adults at Universities and Colleges who was sponsored by their country, either Africa or the West Indies, and who returned after their education was complete. Also, as far as I know most Blacks in education then were men.

My education as far as becoming conscious, that is politically conscious, came mainly through one man and my experience of travelling, not formal school education. That man was Marcus Garvey, and his paper **The Negro World**. Garvey preached of racial pride and change in Africa. He preached about the necessity for educating the Black man, but this education must also be about Black people organising their own business to show that he, the Black man, had the capacity to run his own life. Years ago it was hard for the Black man, no matter what kind of education or skill he had. It is not like today when you could have some Black people in positions. To the Whites (though not all of them) education does not mean a thing, it is the colour of your skin that counts. The education of the Black man is of no consequence to the White man.

The best example of education for the Black man in England happened at the Pan-African Conference in 1944-1945. At this conference many top Black men came from America and Africa and the West Indies. Men like Du Bois, an American educationalist, Nkrumah and Kenyatta from Africa, and Dr. Milliard from the West Indies. The central theme of the conference was education for political change in Africa, but the movement also gave a sort of unity and identity to Blacks in England and other parts of the world. There was no talk as far as I know about the Education Act passed in Parliament at that time as it probably had no significance for Black people. We have always accepted the education system lock, stock, and barrel, and still do. Today it is better because the State helps you through education. For instance, the education of my children could not have occurred without financial help from the State. In the early days you had to be rich to send your child to school. The State provides, regardless of race, it is the administrators and mainly the teachers who are responsible for the racism in education. This situation could be helped, however, by Black parents actively relating with the school. According to law there is no Black or White, the schools are there for both, the administrators must understand this and not misinterpret it.

I have five children and I have devoted my life to giving them the education I did not have. Education is important for the Black people if they are to do well, but it only works when it goes with common sense.

Eldest son.	Age - 30	Joined the British Navy at fifteen and served in the Falklands campaign
Eldest daughter.	- 25	Graduate in Economics from Sussec University (BSc). Now teacher Maths in the Caribbean
Second son.	- 22	An Accountant
Second daughter.	- 19	Completing 'A' levels at South London College
Third daughter.	- 16	'A' levels at South London College

Witnessing the race riots of 1919 in Liverpool and hearing that the same was happening in other British cities, was to raise the level of Mr Marke's awareness of racism.

According to Mr Marke, the Pan-African Conference was a landmark in the political education of Black people in England and abroad.

Mr Marke sincerely believes that in England everybody is equal before the law. To him it is the administrators who give it a rascist interpretation.

CASE HISTORY 3 : TOM BANGBALA

Born in Lagos, Nigeria. Arrived in Liverpool in May 1924, then aged seventeen. A retired electrical engineer. 'A desire to further my education was the reason for coming to England'.

MY FATHER DIED when I was very young and I was brought up by my uncle who supported me through elementary school. He was not able to afford fees for secondary education and it was generally accepted at that time that if anyone wanted a good education, England was the place to go. An opportunity came for me to join a merchant ship to Liverpool as a pantry boy in the Elder Dempster Line.

My early impression of England, the mother country, was influenced by missionaries, 'A lovely place with friendly people'. This view was soon destroyed when I arrived. No jobs for coloured people, except on board ship. No money or advice for further study, and the hostile attitude of the English people was so different from what I had expected. The idea of further education had to be shelved and I rejoined the Elder Dempster Line as a steward for a couple of trips, Lagos to Liverpool run.

A year later I started a correspondence course from Bennett College of Sheffield in Electrical Engineering, while continuing my job aboard ship. Having successfully arrived at a certain stage in the course I felt I was ready and good enough to sit for an exam to gain employment in this firm in Liverpool. I thought this would give me an opportunity to apply my knowledge of theory to a practical situation. I applied to take the exam and included a letter of support from Bennett College. The firm refused my entry, stating that the project was finished some three years ago. I later found out that this was not true. They simply did not want me and I think it was because I was coloured, as they knew my race from my correspondence with them. I still have the letter from them to prove this. I got to the stage where I thought what is the purpose of me using all my energy studying, and I can't get anywhere, except to go to sea? This situation was made worse in that I knew of Whites in the same situation who had no problem of getting jobs. I did not entertain the idea of going back home as I did not want to be thought of as a failure. I continued to go to sea and eventually got married to an English girl (White) in Manchester. At that time there were other coloured people who shared similar experiences, that is, to gain qualifications, only to find that you are unemployable. A friend who introduced me to Bennett College, Mr Galtaugh, completed his Electrical Engineers course and could not get a job, even though there were jobs going. In some ways this whole business of education and employment is strange. The Bennett College motto, 'No one can command success, but everyone can deserve it', don't mean a thing. We deserved it but did not get it.

At that time I knew of no other way of furthering my education or getting a job, so I went back to sea. Whilst at sea I had an accident, lost the sight of one eye, so on return to Manchester I had to find a shore job. After dozens of attempts and a willingness to take any job, I found work on a building site as a hod carrier with Maunders Brothers of Flixton. I was surprised to get this job as no coloured men got jobs ashore. It was said, even by my own people, that I got the job because I used to go to church. All I know was the job was a God-send, especially with my family to keep.

When the war started, some firms were looking for skilled men, as many Whites, both skilled and unskilled, went off to war. I then applied to join the Electrical Trades Union, as it was easier to get a skilled job with a union card. I found out much later that there was some disagreement in accepting me in the union, even though I was a qualified skilled man. The reasons were my colour and doubts about my Bennett College qualification. I was admitted in 1940. The union card gave me an opportunity to gain different working experience. I worked for Dunlops and Metro Vicks (now AEI) both in Trafford Park. Also at Ferranti, Fairy Aviation and the Co-op in Manchester until I retired. In all these jobs I worked as a maintenance engineer. Nineteen years after my arrival in this country I got my final qualifications in Electrical Engineering. I educated myself and took every opportunity to gain practical experience. I could have gone on to further my education but I had a family to keep and no financial assistance, as far as I know, was available. Education did give me the opportunity for some success, though life then was not easy. Because of my experience, especially in the work situation, I became politically conscious and was the first coloured man to join the Labour Party and a trade union in Manchester. I did not, however, participate in Pan-Africanism, as their views were too radical for my taste. They wanted to get things done through aggression, I saw things changing by discussion, through trade unions and by further education of the coloured people of this country. Things must be done in stages. Today more opportunities are open for the coloured people in England, if they make use of it. Things like Adult Education did not exist when I was young as far as I know. Working Men's College came after the war, but in any case I could not have gone because of the shortage of cash. As far as I know, no coloured people went to these institutions, maybe due to lack of money or not knowing what was available, or no encouragement. We, the Missus and me, especially the Missus, did our best for our children's education. They all ended up with a skill and, as far as we know, they had no problems about race at school and the teachers acted O.K. towards them.

Education could do more for coloured people in this country, and needs to do more as the younger generation will not stand for the same treatment as we received.

Eldest son	Age - 50	Draughtsman
Second son	- 45	Welder
Eldest daughter	- 40	Machinist

Seven grand children

Three great grand children

Enrolment on a correspondence course was the only alternative entry into adult education for Mr. Bangbala and others from the Black community domiciled in the United Kingdom. Black people in full and part-time adult education at that time came mainly on sponsored contracts from colonial protectorates. It is interesting to note that participation in correspondence courses was not new to Black people at that time as such courses were already introduced in, and designed for, the colonies. As will be seen in later case studies, the provision of correspondence courses for Black people in the United Kingdom and abroad was to mushroom. Education was seen as the means of financial and social progress, and such courses were the only alternative to secondment or expensive tutorship.

The fact that he could not practice his engineering skills until most men (mainly White) went abroad to war angers Mr Bangbala. He used this issue to make the point that things are better today for coloured people in general, though he acknowledges that there is room for improvement, because as yet, the coloured person is not given the full opportunity to use his qualifications and skills.

An indication of how the political and cultural situation influenced Mr Bangbala's thinking could be seen in his acceptance of the term 'coloured' to describe himself, and members of the Afro-West Indian community, instead of using the word 'Black'. 'Coloured' is a term prescribed by the dominant culture to describe the dominated minority. It denotes expected patterns of behaviour and inter-action between the definer and the definee. The concept 'Black' however, emerges from the group itself and is the result of a struggle for its own identification. This concept also demands changes in the perception and expected patterns of inter-action of the White community to Blacks. It now has near universal acceptance and appeal, and is unique in the sense that the dominant group for the most part has accepted the preference of the dominated group. It is also important to note that the young people are attracted to and accept this label and its implications for consciousness.

A desire to further his education was the reason for Mr Bangbala's decision to emigrate to the U.K.

Racial hostility and unemployment shattered Mr Bangbala's preconceived view of England.

Starting a correspondence course while on board ship was Mr Bangbala's way of entering adult education. This method was favoured by many Black immigrants in that period.

Mr Bangbala took nineteen years to achieve his study aim.

Mr Bangbala found that colour was to influence union membership. A determined effort gave him entry into the union and County Council.

Mr Bangbala refused to participate in Pan-Africanism, as it was too radical.

Things are better today for coloured people, though not good enough for the young, according to Mr Bangbala.

CASE HISTORY 4 : SAMUEL BANGBALA

First son of Mr Thomas Bangbala. Born in Manchester, married with two children. A qualified draughtsman, ex-show business personality and financial adviser.

MY EARLIEST MEMORY of school was that it was interrupted by illness and evacuation due to war. I was then age between five and seven. I cannot remember anyone at that stage, including my teachers, other pupils or those in the area where I lived, reacting to me in any way to do with my race. Though I remember my sister being subjected to racist reactions in the place she stayed at the time of evacuation. We then realised we were different as people used to touch us, because they had not touched a coloured person before. It was not prejudice as the people, especially the children did not know what prejudice was, because in those days so few coloured people lived in England. Prejudice did not exist.

In 1944 I sat and passed high school entrance and went to Dulcie High 1944/1946. I was the only coloured child in that school until 1947, when a couple more coloured children started. Previous to me, I understand that there was one coloured boy there in 1935, he was quite a popular chap. In the school there were Jewish kids who were called 'Yid', and I suppose behind my back they called me 'Nigger', but never to my face. These names were not meant as a slight, they were nicknames. I matriculated in July 1948, wanting to be a professional footballer as I was a good sportsman, but my father would not hear of it. Nothing other than going to learn a trade. My dad influenced my choice of career as there were no careers advice people that I knew of. I wrote off for apprenticeships to various firms and went to some interviews. In one particular company in Trafford Park, which made electrical motors and alternators, they told me it would be difficult to get an apprenticeship, as they did not take on coloured people. I then had an interview with Metropolitan-Vickers in Trafford Park who ran a school for their apprentices. In that school they trained students from all over the world - Ceylon, Africa, India, Brazil and so on. There was no racism at Vickers, as it was an international company. I was taken on as an apprentice electrical engineer, the same trade as my dad.

I had a successful apprenticeship because I worked very hard. I joined the Apprenticeship Association (a kind of union), and held all the offices of the Association to Vice-Chairmanship. I then entered the race to be elected as Chairman, a result which was supposed to be a foregone conclusion, but then I had my first conscious experience of prejudice. My so-called friends who I expected to support me, did not. It was my first experience of going so far and having the door shut in my face because I was coloured. While an apprentice I won the official apprentice shield given to the most able apprentice, and winning it allowed me a further two years training in administration. On completion of that two years further study I was offered the chance to join the company's drawing department, to be an electrical draughtsman. I left Vickers at the age of thirty and went to a firm of contract draughtsmen as it was a better job. I enjoyed my time with this firm. Looking back, it was during my apprenticeship that I began to feel the pressure of prejudice in this country. At that time lots more coloured people were coming into the country. This was after the war and there was a change of attitude regarding the coloureds, especially in places like Moss Side. Bigotry had started to creep in, even in my personal life, in that it influenced my girl friends' fathers' attitude to me. As more coloured people came into the country prejudice grew, though it was not a mass type of bigotry, but individuals response to the situation. This bigotry came not from the older generation, but from the young ones coming home after the war. They had experience of African and Egyptian peoples, and they used the word 'wog' to describe coloured people. Incidentally, 'wog' means worthy oriental gentleman. It is not a derogatory term.

My schooling, further education and career was heavily influenced by my dad. I remember when I was about four years old, my dad studying night after night to get his qualifications and this influenced me. To him, education came first. He used to say 'Get that background, a skill behind you, and you will never go wrong'. He was right. He brought us up with an iron hand, but both are very kind parents who gave us everything they could. They went out of their way to see us through. I have not been back in education since the time of my training, but what I learnt has stood me in good stead throughout my life. It gave me an insight not only into engineering, but to other areas of life as well.Schooling brought me out, made me more extrovert, especially in sports. The then headmaster of Dulcie High, Mr Taylor, was a fine gentleman and I got a very good impression of all my teachers, except Mr Cresswell who, in my second year made some derogatory remarks about me in front of the class which upset me. I reported this to my mother who went to the school and sorted things out. My mother always fought our school battles, while my father more or less advised us on the work situation, trade unions and that.

In my school days and as an apprentice you always did as you were told, discipline was the first and last thing that you learnt. You were strongly reprimanded and everybody accepted it, even if it meant the cane in school. Teachers attitude to dress and professional behaviour was adult. Today these factors seem not to be there, to be unimportant. Discipline and respect are thrown out of the window, and children go so far as to do physical harm to teachers. Discipline must be enforced as in that way, education will be able to influence the majority on racism, as children will be taught the way they ought to be taught. In my day if you did not want to learn you were forced to; today we let children do as they want to. As a result there seems to be more illiteracy. Exam results are proof of this, as at fifteen years of age many can't read or write. Part of the reason for this is the children's home life. The majority of mothers go out to work and the children look after themselves. In my day the majority of women stayed at home.

Attitudes on race, even in schools, has got worse. At Ducie I was the only coloured child of about five hundred children. The environment was such that there was no threat, but when there is a 60% Black and 40% White situation, as it now is, then there must be conflict. Racism occurs when numbers present a threat, people basically do not understand, and the multiplying of the coloured people in this country since the fifties has not helped. Enoch Powell's observation is correct, we have too many coloured people in this country. When you have the majority of coloured in one school, then the coloured man is a threat. Not only to White children, but to White parents. To my mind, anybody will tolerate a minority, but not a majority. You know, even being born in this country you are seen as an immigrant? I was born here, I am English, but anybody seeing me will say, there goes another nigger off a banana boat. He does not know that I was born in this country.

This feeling of my situation came with mass immigration. Some of the things you read in the newspapers today, you could not find in the early days. Because of this, there will be a lot of trouble in this country. Not necessarily caused by the Black man, nor the White man, but by subversive elements, the Communists and the National Front, who want an excuse to cause havoc. The riots last summer are an example of this. The Black man was used by communist infiltrators. Education could certainly help, but it's going to be a struggle.

COMMENT

MR SAMUAL BANGBALA

Unprofessional teacher attitudes, lack of discipline in the schools and home, linked with mothers. It is interesting to note that such views form the centrepiece of the 'Black Papers on Education', edited by Professors Cox and Dyson. To Samuel, racism is really prejudice and not attributable to antipathy; not social but psychological in origin. To him this phenomenon is ignited by the large numbers of Black immigrants, who represent a threat to the status quo. Samuel is supportive of Mr Powell's ideas on the subject, and extends this view further by linking the issue of race and education to subversion by communist elements in society.

His early schooling was influenced by war and illness, but was otherwise happy and constructive. Racism, so often reported as a feature of Black schooling in the United Kingdom, was not part of Samuel's experience. 'Prejudice did not exist in England then'. Samuel was among the first Black pupils to gain an advantage from the 1944 Education Act. He matriculated at the time the programme of educational change got off the ground. His schooling led to an apprenticeship, following rejections from many training institutions on grounds of his colour.

An important aspect of Samuel's education and training was the role his parents played. He saw their participation as essential to his progress, suggesting that it be recorded. Samuel reports the school as not having a careers service. He therefore depended on his father to perform that role, and it is no wonder he followed in his father's footsteps initially. His father's long nights of study were also influential in forming Samuel's attitude to school work. Samuel's mother's role was to sort out any problems he encountered at school. Together they provided a very positive input. It is not surprising however, that some of Samuel's responses resembles those of his father's. They both favour structured change, both use the word 'coloured' in the same context; as does his mum. And Samuel supports his father's view that there was no racism at school.

CASE HISTORY 5 : RAYMOND BANGBALA

Second son of Mr Thomas Bangbala. Born in Manchester; occupation welder.

UNLIKE MY ELDER brother my early schooling was uneventful.I was the only non-White child in West Grove Primary in Chorlton-on-Medlock at that time. My relationship with the teachers and pupils was quite good. I may have been called names but it was never seen as insulting at this stage. I also failed my eleven plus exam, as I had no real interest in school work, and when I went on to Secondary Modern School I became aware of racial differences, and met insults from other children which, quite often ended in fights. The children who 'called' me did not know me from Primary School, and they really made me realise that I was different compared to them. I feel that children today are more aware, as they are subjected to issues about race on T.V. and sometimes at school. My work improved slightly while at Secondary School and my relationship with both staff and students, on the whole, were good. On one occasion though, the Woodwork Teacher did not give me an opportunity to produce work which I felt happened because of my colour. I reacted angrily by throwing a piece of work at the teacher, and was sent up before the Headmaster. The head, Mr Ashley, understood after hearing my story; he was very fair and did not punish me. At the end of the year I was top of the woodwork course because the incident made me determined to do well. I suppose the education I got at school was O.K., even though I was not very good academically, I am good with my hands. In fact I learnt more when I left school than when I was at school.

I left school without any qualifications and went into further education at the College of Building in Manchester, as a day-release student. I wanted to be a plumber, and my dad and mum supported me. My mum took me to see the careers person in Manchester, and he told me that apprenticeships for coloured young people was harder to get than apprenticeships for White lads. He told me that if he got me fixed up, I will have to learn as much as I can and to do, not equally well as my White counterparts, but twice as well as them if I am to get on. Though my parents influenced me, they really allowed me to choose my career and I got this sponsored apprenticeship with the Manchester Housing Association in Burnage. I obtained my City and Guilds Certificate in plumbing, casting and arc welding and this was the first time I took an interest in the theory side of education.

When I completed my apprenticeship I wanted to learn more, and felt that I could not go as far as I wanted to with the Housing Association so, with the help of my union I was able to get release from my contract with the Housing Association. While at college I found the teachers there to be better than those at school. They had experience in the trade and I knew that I was involved in something that was going to be useful to me. On leaving the Housing Association I joined Shell and stayed with them for about six years. While there I did not continue my formal education as there was enough to keep me interested, doing different jobs. While I was at Shell I came up against the most prejudice, especially from the foremen who gave the coloured guys the 'bum' jobs; it was only if you kicked up a fuss would you get a good job. I left Shell to work for a firm of contractors and at the same time enrolled at Stretford Technical College on an evening class for a course in industrial welding. I was successful in this, and while there met a teacher who used to be at the College of Building. He told me of a new advanced course (Course 90) an offer at the College of Building and advised me to apply for a place in it, promising to support my application. I did as suggested and passed the course with distinction, getting an award on the way. While at college this second time, I found that my fellow students did not take too well the view that I was doing better than they. I was the subject of many taunts even though I was not trying to prove I was better, but that I was a good craftsman who liked job satisfaction. My attitude was influenced by what the careers officer told me years before, though at the time it did not have much impact. Once I understood the meaning of his words it gave me dignity. I try to do things well not because I am a coloured man, but because I am a good craftsman.

I now had all the qualifications going in my field and lots of experience, yet I did not get into any senior positions. I know myself that I was never power mad, as I have seen the attitude of some bosses and I can't be like that. I feel that my colour influenced my promotion chances as I have seen White blokes get senior positions, who were useless. Generally firms do not, in my experience, promote coloured folks in the trade. Some White blokes do not like to work with a coloured foreman. In this trade you tend to know the tradesmen in your area who tend to accept you, it is more the strangers in the trade who resent coloured foremen. Personally, no matter how good you are I don't think the coloured person will ever get an equal chance; they may say nice things but that's all, no matter how educated you are. Education cannot really alter people's attitude; it is a good thing, but at the end of the day all the pieces of paper they give you is useless if you are now allowed to apply it.

I did well enough in my education to be invited to go into teaching my skills, but it doesn't appeal to me. Today, there seems to be far more prejudice than when I was young, even though children and grown-ups are more aware of race. I personally don't think prejudice will ever end; it may be in people's nature. The coloured child will now get the opportunities he deserves because of this.

Secondary education meaningless.   Raymond left school 'empty handed'.   He learnt more when he left school.

Raymond attended day-release class at Further Education College.   Class work enjoyed for the first time.

Raymond discovers that colour counts more than skills in opportunities for promotion.

Racism found to be more extensive today than when Raymond was at school.

CASE HISTORY 6 : AUDREY WILKIE

Born in Manchester, a machinist and the only daughter of
Mr Tom Bangbala.

MY ONLY CLEAR memory of my primary schooling was that
I knew everybody was going to look and stare at me. I
knew this from going out with my mam when people turned
around and stared. Though a bit unsure, I still looked
forward to going to school. When I got there I found that
I was the only coloured girl there, and my elder brother
Sammy was the only coloured boy there. I remember that I
was not successful at eleven plus, because girls weren't
pushed and I did not know I was taking an important exam.
I went to Modern School 'til I was fourteen years of age,
and while there I remember being evacuated during the war.
People then were not nasty to me, they only looked as
though they never saw anybody coloured before. Like a
novelty, they touched my hair and asked silly questions.

At school I got on well with all the teachers and was quite popular. When I left school I got a good report and got a job as a machinist. I did not really want to do machining but my mam said it was a good steady job. Anyway, it was the only job for people like me to go to. We could not get jobs in shops or offices and that, and I did not want to go any further in education, as I wanted to earn a living.

At school, I did not get any careers help like you get today. I had to decide what I wanted to do with my parents' help. My parents chose my career, though I did not turn out too bad. When I got married I wanted to change jobs and went to Dolcis, the shoe people in Manchester. They had just opened this new shop and I heard they were taking coloured people. I was the first coloured person to be employed in the city centre shop. While at this job I used to wish I had done something else, even taking a further course in education; but then we did not have the opportunities to go back to education like you have today. Alright, you may not be able to get a job, but at least you are told what you can do and how to go about it.

One of my teachers asked me what I wanted to do when I left school and hinted to my mam that I would make a good nursery teacher, but that's as far as that went. Careers advice from my experience seemed to be for those pupils who were successful at eleven plus, especially boys, and if you were White. To me that was the real distinction. I felt that there were lots of careers I would have liked to get information on, but did not receive any. Nursing was one of them, though I felt that personally I might not make a good nurse, as I would get emotionally involved in the patients' problems. Teaching also attracted me but it was for people up the ladder in society and all of them were White.

My mom and dad showed interest in my education and career but seemed more keen on making sure of my brothers' education, as when my brothers get married they will have to be the provider for their family. I was told that if I was ever stuck, machining will come in handy. I also had no confidence, and used to think that something was wrong with me; still, I would have liked to be part of some business where I could meet lots of people and get a bit more confident. I have tried to pass on my experience and ideas to my daughter and tell her to try and do the things she wants to do, but she is not very confident. My sons have not done too badly, both had training and Peter played professional football.

Audrey's views are more closely related to her father's and elder brother's, than to those of Raymond, her younger brother. The startling contrast in experience is accounted for by the sex difference. A trend is perpetuated in her. In passing on her ideas and experience to her daughter, in the family style, she maintains the tradition of the orthodox family role. Audrey's only daughter, aged nineteen, was unwilling to participate in this research project, as she felt too shy to be involved. Audrey stated that her daughter did not speak much, and that when she does it is mainly to members of the family. She was said to have got nothing from the school system that enabled her to fashion her own life. She has never been employed, except for a very short training spell in hairdressing. She gave this up as she found it difficult to relate to customers. She is not enthusiastic to pursue further training or employment due to her lack of confidence in herself, but would like to be able to do so. While education is highly thought of as a mechanism for success by Audrey, it has failed to perform a positive role for these two Black women.

No careers service for Blacks, and very few careers for Black girls, according to Audrey.

First Black person to work in retail shop in Central Manchester; but Audrey was not satisfied with this.

CASE HISTORY 7 : PETER WILKIE

Born in Manchester, eldest son of Mrs Wilkie, and grandson of Mr Tom Bangbala. An ex-professional footballer and insurance salesman; at present a plumber.

I WAS THE only Black person in my Primary School and remember being called names by the older children. That did not really bother me. The teachers treated me like all the other kids, and I was beginning to become very popular due to my sporting ability. All I remember the teacher saying to me was that I probably could get to Grammar School; though they advised me against it, as they felt that I would not work hard enough at it. I did take my eleven plus and failed and I felt this linked up with the teacher's statement on my keenness. I think the teachers knew me well. At twelve years of age I went to boarding school in the south. The opportunity came due to my sporting ability and was sponsored by the local Education Authority. I stayed at that school for two

years and while there, got on well with both the teachers
and the other kids. There was one other Black lad in the
school. I returned to Manchester with the hope of joining
Manchester City Football Club, but did not make the grade.

I went back to school in Manchester and got called by
the other kids, but again I seemed to get most of them on
my side due to my involvement in sports, especially
soccer. I gained respect of most people in the school and
even became slightly popular. I never got encouraged in
any way by the teachers as though they had it in for me.
Looking back on it now, I know that I did better than some
of the other students, but never got on. I had a similar
experience when I went for the Lancashire Boys football
trials. I did well, but again I never made it. I was
told it was because of my size; what I did not know then
and know now is that these things happened to me because
I was Black. There were a few Black lads every year for
trials and none ever made it, even though some of them
were really good. I found out much later that there was a
saying in football that Black players had no heart. I got
that from a football manager.

When I left school without any qualifications I went
to Oldham Athletic Football Club. I would have liked a
bit more schooling but no one ever pushed me, there was no
interest in me. I felt that if I was pushed I would have
done better, as my school exam marks were always near the
top of the class. While at Oldham I was given day release
to attend Further Education College. I went to Bury to
take a course in plumbing (City and Guilds). I knuckled
down, did the work, and passed with distinction. The
students at College did not act prejudically to me, as I
was one of the boys and could take care of myself. The
students tended to pick on the Pakistani lads as they could
not look after themselves. The teachers often made
remarks about race in a joking manner, but it was a dig at
Blacks.

During my Football League career, I very often felt
that I played well, scoring goals, but I never got beyond
the 'B' team. When I did not make it in full-time
football I tried part-time professional soccer and at the
same time, tried to get a job selling. Getting a job
selling was not easy, as I wrote dozens of applications
but never got further than a first interview. Quite often
the interviewer informed me of the problem of having

coloured salesmen, but never indicated that this would influence the situation. I never got second interviews, or jobs. Due to this disappointment I went back into the plumbing trade as, at that time, there was a heavy housing programme. The people I worked with in the plumbing trade generally treated me O.K. except one bloke, and that may be due to a clash of personalities. While in plumbing, I tried to get time off to go back to College and was fired when I made my request. I took my case to the union, they promised to look into it, but nothing was ever done.

I went back into football with Boston United and it was the manager of this club who, earlier on, told me about the attitudes to Black players in the Football League. I stayed for twelve months and then moved to Telford United where a famous England player was later appointed manager. My worst experience of racism was from this new manager. Prejudice in football is never by your own team mates, it is always by the opposition and their supporters. In this case with the new manager I was playing really well, scoring lots of goals when I did get a game. He continued to give me a hard time for no reason, and when I enquired I was told by one of the senior players that he did not like Black people. At the end of the season he threatened to release me from my contract, stating that an American club came in for me, which never materialised. I stayed at Telford playing mainly in the reserves for a further year.

I then went into selling with the help of my uncle and during this time I took the opportunity to learn as much as I could of the insurance game. I was then offered full-time soccer in America with Baltimore Blast, and got injured while playing there, and this injury - cartilage - ended my football career.

I feel that education could be helpful in cutting out racism, but only if teachers pushed Black students to do well. Now that my career in football has ended I've gone back at this late stage into education under the government scheme doing something in the plumbing field. If I'd had the support from school earlier on I would not be in this situation now.

Between twelve and eighteen years of age, Peter's life was almost totally dominated by football.

Another attempt to make a career in football fails. Peter returns to being a tradesman and again re-enters the education system.

Education seen as central to success. Peter is especially impressed with the arrangements for 'second-chance'.

CASE HISTORY 8 : RAYMOND WILKIE

The second son of Mrs Wilkie and grandson of Mr Tom
Bangbala Sr. Born in Manchester, Raymond is an ex-painter
and decorator and semi-professional musician. Presently
unemployed.

MY SCHOOLING WAS not really all that important. I
lost interest in school work very early on because the
teachers lost interest in me. There were other Blacks in
both Primary and Secondary School, and also Chinese
students. In the third year of Secondary School we had to
choose to do either CSE or GCE's. I was advised against
GCE's but I had planned to leave school the Easter of my
sixteenth birthday anyway, so I did not put much effort
into anything. Anyway, if I had taken either CSE or GCE
exams I would have been too old to get an apprenticeship.
Because I was not taking any exams the teachers did not
try to persuade me; they gave up. So from then onwards
school was a waste of time for me. I wanted a welding

apprenticeship and I had to go looking for it myself. We did have careers people coming around at school, but they never seemed to help anybody get jobs. The school did not help me and I reckon I learnt more out of school than I did in school. In school we had no confidence in our teachers and this was due to the lack of discipline in the place. We were allowed to do as we pleased. I was really interested in music at school but was not encouraged, so I taught myself to play the drums. The music teacher was only interested in Beethoven and stuff like that. I was not interested in that type of music. My parents bought me a second-hand drum kit on which I learnt.

Another reason for my lack of progress at school was related to people's view of the school and this included the pupil's view. Everybody knew the school was rubbish, a bad school. What they taught us was not useful in that it was no use to us after we left school, and that is what we were interested in. To me it is not education in this country that is bad, but certain schools and teachers. The teachers gave us no direction at all, because when at school I was too young to know what I really wanted to do, other than music, and the teachers never put any ideas in my mind. I could remember lessons where we messed around with tadpoles for no reason at all. I still to this day don't know why we did those things. The students in the 'A' stream had some teachers interested in them, but not us. The Maths teacher was a bit different though, she took an interest in us. I did not like her at first, but when we did badly in the mock exams she went mad. In the real exam most of us did really well and I came top. After that we all really liked her. I went to Secondary Modern School having failed my eleven plus. Only six children passed out of sixty or so from our Primary School. At Secondary School there was one teacher who always picked on me; a Mr Hampton, who taught Social Studies, even though I was never in any serious trouble at school, like 'wagging it'. I would have liked the teachers to be more strict with me and the others, to tell us what to do and what was going to be useful when we left school.

My mum cared very much about my schooling, but she always trusted and believed in the school and what the teachers said. Racial prejudice was not that important in my school life. I was called names by both Blacks and

Whites . The Black students called me 'half baked' and on
one occasion my White friends said 'Look at them niggers
over there'. I said to them I was Black as well, and they
said I was not like them, that I was different. It makes
you really wonder about this race thing. When I left
school I got a painter/decorator apprenticeship through my
own efforts. I really wanted a welding apprenticeship but
could not get one. I did not finish my apprenticeship as
the firm folded up. I then took another job painting
(maintenance work) with another firm, but gave that up to
go to America as a drummer with a dance band. Since
coming back to England I have been a semi-professional
musician.

I have never thought of going back into education to
do any sort of course as it is a waste of time. There are
too many people coming out of education qualified and
can't get jobs, and even if you get a good education,
people like me won't get the real opportunities anyway.
If I did go back for any course it would be for my
personal satisfaction. For example, if I had the chance
again I would take music lessons and try to go to a music
school, even if that meant having to get GCE's. A lot of
people from my school did not achieve anything, both
Blacks and Whites, but more so Blacks. The girls got wed,
a couple of White lads joined the Police Force. Another
lad got a job with a tour company selling package holidays
and some went into welding and engineering. Few Blacks
got into engineering, but that was all, the rest just
drifted.

COMMENT

The idea of being involved in a system that educates is a good one. It is the practice of education that is unacceptable. This point is made very succinctly by Raymond when he stated, 'To me, it is not the education in this country that is bad but schools and teachers'. Raymond's entire school experience is seen as insignificant. He reports himself as having learnt more out of school than in it.

Lack of discipline was a point stressed in his catalogue of evidence. Also, that the teachers favoured the academically orientated student and paid little attention to others was a disappointment to him. As in many of the other case studies, one teacher is remembered for his/her ability to communicate, understand, and make a positive contribution to the pupils' education. In Raymond's case it was the Maths teacher. The negative view of school held by its pupils extended to the community it served, yet Raymond reports his parents', especially his mother's continued trust in the school. This may be a way of demonstrating the respect that people extend to accredited institutions and the professionals who work in them. It could be that there is lack of information available to the public on how to correct bad situations in schools: it is more politic simply to hope for change. This view may rest on the fear that challenging the system could do more harm than good to the education of their child. Raymond's observation that pupils 'drifted' at the end of their secondary schooling confirms his view that the activities at school had little relevance to life outside it. It also noted the absence of a positive careers service and suggests the existence of a teaching staff isolated from the community, both inside the school and outside it.

Raymond's experience has turned him off any further participation in education, especially vocational training. Vocational education is still seen as irrelevant to his everyday experience, and being Black does not endear him to a system that occupationally disenfranchises people like himself.

His schooling at both primary and secondary levels is not seen as significant by Raymond.

Raymond is unlikely to re-enter the education system.

CASE HISTORY 9 : TOMMY BANGBALA

Son of Mr Sammy Thomas Bangbala and grandson of Mr Tom Bangbala. Occupation, musician - first violinist with the B.B.C. Northern Symphony Orchestra. Born in England, age twenty five.

I **AM NOT** visibly Black and this influenced my total school experience. Because of this I experienced no racism at school. I do have somewhat foreign appearance, but no one is sure where to place me. In primary school my surname aroused intrigue, and recognising this was my earliest experience that I was different, everyone wanting to know where the name came from. This however, was not a disadvantage, and difficult to explain. For had I been visibly Black, things would be of a different perspective. I might have taken comments made in a totally different way. At school there were other Blacks and some kids of Indian and Pakistani parentage. I do recall one Black pupil, Derek Nivens, who was of Jamaican stock, and a very close friend, but as far as I know at that early age, it was difficult for us as children to recognise racism. Maybe it is different these days as so much emphasis is placed on race, but when I was a boy this was not part of my thinking. I never had racial feeling to anybody else, and they never had towards me. As far as I know Derek did not have a different experience to me in that sense, neither from students or teachers. We were not conscious of race when at primary school, though we were often disciplined for high spirits, not because of our race. I identified with Derek, not because of his race, but that we got on well. At that time differences were placed more on accents than on colour, and the only student who got ragged on this was a pupil who was originally from Egypt. I suppose this ragging could be seen as a basis for racism. The staff and students knew of my parental background, a Black father and a White mom: though they never saw my dad as he left home by the time I was nine. My mom always fought my battles.

The eleven plus was abolished the year before I finished my fourth year. I went to Burnage High which used to be Grammar and merged with Ladybarn Secondary. I found the Grammar school teachers in the comprehensive far more use than the secondary school teachers in my first three years. The teachers were always kind to me, they were always willing to bend over backwards to help me. I never had a teacher who had it in for me. I was a bit wild at the expense of school work and that was from the influence of the kids around me. We were all of different backgrounds, mixed races etc. I took up the violin in the second year and that made me a lot more serious, though my academic work was terrible. It was not until the fourth year in the type of Grammar school atmosphere that the teachers made me knuckle down to work. The teachers had that certain air of authority that I did not object to and which helped me. The headmaster once said of me, 'You bludgeoned your way through school', which I thought was an interesting thing to say.

Though having a Nigerian name my background has been geared to living on the White side and therefore I have a totally different experience than other members of my family on my father's side had had. I am the only one who appears White, my cousins are all half-caste, whereas I am quarter-caste. My name is the only thing that arouses interest, a name that no one remembers and no one forgets. During my post-school education (College of Music) my name aroused intrigue, they (teachers and students) found it exotic and did not know where to place it, whereas if I was Black they would have placed it immediately, as African. My name would not have the significance it does now. Some people even think I look Spanish. What I did notice was that many of the Black kids at school (secondary) were in the lower classes, some in remedial, and they were always getting into trouble. There was no direct racism, at least none that I could see. What interested me when I went on to music college, was that there was only one Black student there, a chap called Roy, who also played the violin. It interests me to know why there are not many Black people in classical music, except some in the States, because it is a very music-orientated race.

In the music profession there are always jokes and jokers. If there are any comments made about Blacks - though to say 'Blacks' sounds so immediately racial - any jokes about the jungle, whatever, are immediately directed at me, and I play up on this because, one, I am not ashamed of having a background that is Black. Comments passed are not racist, though maybe it would be different if I was visibly Black. I do not identify consciously with Blacks or Whites, and I do not have strong views about anything in particular. It's something of my live and let live attitude. The only thing I identify with is music, and this may be because music is an international language. For example, our orchestra hosted an Argentinian pianist during the Falklands war, and there was no animosity on either side. I suppose this type of thing colours my view. I am not unaware of the Black and White issues that exist, but I don't think, Oh! there's a Black person, I must relate to them.

I gained a lot from my schooling, yes, what I am today. School influenced my choice of career, especially the music teacher. As far as I know there is no history of classical music in the family, but while at school I loved going to the Halle and watching the older kids at school play the violin. This music teacher intrigued me so much I just had to stick with him and learn, even though sometimes I wanted to give up. It was as if I was talking to sombody from the past, and this fostered my interest in the fiddle. From then on the violin was the most important thing in my life. I practiced day in day out, and spent most evenings in the central library (music section) learning of the instrument. I however ended up wanting to make violins, not to play and wrote to Hills in London for a job. They wrote back and said they would not take me because I did not live in London. Now, thinking of it, that was an interesting point, because that was their excuse; whether it was true or not I do not know. Now, had I been visibly Black I might have thought, is it because I am Black they did not give me that chance? but it never occurred to me they could recognise the name or check with my school, or anything like that. It is a bit of a weak excuse really, not living in London. You see what I'm trying to get at? I was prepared to move to London, that's why I wrote off to them. It is that one criteria, just a different colour of pigmentation of skin, how silly, it's stupid really. Very often when I meet with people who know my name but never met me they often say they expected me to be Black or foreign. Often when I write letters I often wonder what the recipients think of my name. I wanted to alter my name when dad left home, as mom was having a bad time. I hated dad and hated the name, but mom did not want me to change it. The name also made me stand out at school, and kids do not like to stand out, they want to be part of a group, and my name made me stand out. I thought I'd rather be called Smith or something. Having got over adolescence my name has been nothing but an advantage, it stands out in an orchestral list. It's such a distinctive name, I love it.

My route to post-school education and a career in music, is really the encouragement I got from my violin teacher and my mum. He saw my potential and insisted I entered for a junior exhibition. I gained a scholarship given by the education committee, and applied to students from low income background. I went on to do fairly well at college and while there I met Martin Millner, the leader of the Halle Orchestra, who became my tutor and had a lot of influence on my career. Other than that, the school played an indirect part in pointing to my career, in that they provided me with the opportunity to play the violin. The local authority's careers chap visited us and when I told him I wanted to be a violinist, he said 'Oh! well, I see. Well I am not really the chap to talk to'.

He then said 'Have you tried music college?' That was all. He probably thought that I was over ambitious, but I realised that he could not help me. While at college, I noticed only one other Black person there, a lad, who played the bassoon. I did not have a lot of contact with him as he was younger than I, and in another group. As far as I know he made it too.

At work my colleagues know that I am part Black, and although they never come out and say it they find me somewhat the centre of attraction. I can see it's gone through their minds; that it is unusual that someone from my background, my race, has got this far. As far as I know there is only one Black pianist called Rita Barrow and a Black soloist, named Edmund Reid (they are both Americans, I think). I may be the only first violinist in the country that is Black. Even though I am not Black of skin, my appearance obviously influences people's way of talking to me. They do make jokes and comments knowing my background, but if anybody makes a racial comment that they mean, I let them know; and they don't make the same mistake twice. I am very conscious of that, and I suppose it is my identification with being Black. I don't hide my roots. So far, racism has not seriously affected my career. Like school, music college was non-racist. Most of my teachers there were foreign, though White, but music is so mixed anyway. Racial domination does not exist as it may do in, say, engineering.

Tom attended multi-racial schools at both primary and secondary levels. Dialect, not race, was the identifying factor.

Tom attended a Comprehensive School, but was able to recognise teachers with a Grammar School background.

CASE HISTORY 10 : MUNIRU FARO

Born in Lagos, Nigeria. Sixty four years of age. Occupation, technical technician. Came to England to further studies in his field.

ALL MY EARLY schooling and apprenticeship took place in Nigeria. 1942 presented me with an opportunity for further studies and to respond, like many other colonials, to the call for an effort against Hitler. I thought that after doing my bit in the war I would enrol for a further course in my trade. I had experience of seafaring while working in the Nigerian Royal Navy, travelling mainly between Nigeria and South Africa, but switched to the Merchant Navy in order to get to England. At that time the Elder Dempster shipping line was the main merchant agency to employ Black seamen. On arrival things were very different than I expected and was told. For example, opportunities for education was there, but to afford it, you had to get a job, and that was not easy. It was a struggle to live. I registered at Bennett College for a correspondence course but this did not work for me as, during the war we had what is called an emergency work order. This meant that I, like other workers, could be kept in the factory for many days. They used to give us drugs to keep us awake so that we could work, though they said the stuff they gave us was to keep us fit. I also found out that much of the material that Bennett College sent me as part of the course was the same we had in Nigeria, so because of these two factors I gave up the course.

I proved my skill -much of it which I learned back home - by working at Massey Ferguson, who made engines for aeroplanes. I worked there as a skills instructor. This was at the time of the lease lend scheme, i.e.lending machines to equip other factories and train their workers. I got a job as a skills instructor to a group of women. Though I had the ability and knowledge to do the job, I only got it because in those days most of the White men went off to war, so the employers took anybody who could do these jobs. They called us 'dilutees'. When the war was over we were kicked out of those jobs. Not only that, but did you know that even the boys, Black boys who went to war for this country, for example in the R.A.F. -and some rose to Flying Officer rank - got a hard time after the war? This information was never mentioned in dispatches, all the war films made to glorify the men, never portray Black faces. They never talk about what our people did for this country, and this angers me. The Whites in this country are brainwashed in such a way, that when they see you as a coloured person, if you show any bit of intelligence, they say Oh!! you're an American Negro, second a West Indian, and then an African - an idiot - as the African may have gone to mission school. We have to teach these people that intelligence and learning is not limited to one place or race, and its people like you researchers who have the opportunity to do this. To my surprise, on arriving in England I found that there were a lot of Whites who were illiterate, and there were Whites who were really poor. Sometimes both together. I found it hard to believe at first, from the stories we hear from the White man about England. After

the war I kept working and did not at that stage go back
to further my education. As a skilled man I joined the
union and had no problems being accepted. I did my time
in the union and rose to branch chairman.

During the Pan-African Conference in Manchester
(1945) I was an official representing the Negro
Association of Manchester. This was an association
functioning for the interest of Black people and formed in
1942.   At the Pan-African Conference itself, political
education was emphasised. That is, the fight for freedom
and dignity for Black people through consciousness to
obtain independence for countries like India and Africa,
but also for respectability for Black people all over the
world.   Foremost among the delegates was Nkrumah from
Ghana - then called the Gold Coast. He was a very clever
man, a visionary, a philosopher and educator.   Jomo
Kenyatta of Kenya was also there, though he was a more
fiery man, an emotional speaker. It is interesting to
note, and not much has been said of this, but many of the
leaders at that conference later became heads of their
governments on independence or held senior positions.
That conference was a crucial step in the education and
change in the lives of Black people all over the world.
If it was a White man's conference that achieved as much
the world would've heard more of it.

No matter what we do we never get any credit unless
it is about crime. A very close friend of mine, Mr
Asuma, was in the Merchant Navy during the war and saw
action in the South American campaign against the Bismark.
When he arrived back after the war he lost his job as a
seaman, which was given to a White person. He took
advantage of a government training scheme for ex-
servicemen and chose to take hairdressing from a list of
trades offered. He did a little hairdressing in Ghana and
on board ship, and wanted to learn to cut European hair
properly. He got a lot of trouble from the training
instructors because of his race and had to use his savings
to train privately. This story is just to indicate the
problems Blacks had in getting good training if they
decided on adult education. While my friend was going
through that, I was out of a job and found that the many
interviews I went to as a skilled man, instead of saying
they did not want you because you were Black, they changed
the requirements of the job from what was originally

advertised, and asked you if you could do a bit of this and that. You know, as a fitter they will ask me, can you do welding?, can you do blacksmiths work? plus what you have been trained for. They knew damn well that's wrong, wanting me to do three people's work for one wage. It was also a ploy for not employing Black men, as they never asked the White men to do the same. In the end I went back to further my education in welding through training at a skills centre, and experienced a lot of frustration, in that they tried to prevent me from progressing by withholding information which I had to find out for myself. They also made it difficult for me to get practice of using the equipment by saying, the equipment was in use at the time. I left and went to another skills centre in Wigan to learn central lathe turning. Here too I found resentment and inadequate instruction. I began to blame myself and thought I asked too many questions, and sometimes I challenged the instructor's analysis of a situation.

Many Blacks went to skills centres after the war though as far as I know no Blacks had the opportunity to go to university at that time. The only Blacks who went to university were from abroad and came through colonial scholarships. We knew what was going on, realising that if you were Black you got training for less important jobs. Whites never liked the idea of Blacks being better qualified or suited than them. It is true, in theory, that everybody has an equal opportunity in education, but in my experience this is not true in practice. For example it is like giving us British citizenship in theory, but when we try to claim it in practice, we have to fight for it. I believe education can be a way to ease tension and raise the status of the Black man, but unlike the Indians, we have lost our heritage, language, and religion. We have replaced it with something foreign, and seem to regard theirs as better than what we had. Before Europeans arrived in Africa, religion and government were flourishing and pre-dates western tradition. A look at western civilisation will shows its African influence as members of the Greek intelligentsia, like Homer, boasted of Negro blood.

The education of Black people must begin with our history and a pride in it. We must demand it and make good use of it. I know that a number of Black people get qualifications and cannot get a job to suit their

education, but as a group we must continue to pursue
education and be ready to play our part in this country,
which is ours too.   The way things are going there will
come a time when both races will have to get it together,
or sink together.   What my generation tolerated, this
young Black generation will not.   They know their rights,
they are English and feel English, and that is important,
because they then feel they have a right to share
everything in this society.   Education could open our eyes
to the injustices and how to deal with them.   We may not
get the opportunities we deserve, but with education we
can be made aware of how to obtain it.

Pan-Africanism and the development of Black consciousness were significant for him.

Unemployment after war. The change of job specifications as an employer's evasive device.

Blacks unable to obtain occupation to match their qualifications.

CASE HISTORY 11 : KATH LOCKE

I WAS BORN in Manchester of a Nigerian father and English (White mother, and I am employed as a community organiser for the W.E.A. I experienced a strong Catholic influence from birth and, influenced by my father, I gained a spiritual link with Africa and the history and life of Black people in England. My father arrived in England in 1909 at the age of twelve. He was a ship's cabin boy, could not read nor write in English, and adopted the name of the ship's captain. A common feature of African seamen in England at that time. I spent the early years of my life in Whalley Range, a few miles from the city centre of Manchester. We were the only Black family in the area and like most of the kids of the neighbourhood I went to the Catholic nursery school. My memories of it was an unhappy school experience, the other kids did not play with me, it was like looking in at something you could not get into. My earliest happy experience was when my father took me to other Black families and I saw other people who looked like myself.

That opened the door for me. I remember my mother making the most beautiful parties for me and nobody would come. I thought something was wrong with me. When I was six years old my mother was very poorly so we went to live in Blackpool as it was healthier. The first school I went to in Blackpool was a very happy school and it might have been because it was not a Catholic School. I was sent there while awaiting a place at the Catholic school, and while at this school I was brought into all activities of the school. Later I went on to the Catholic school and that was the end of a happy experience. I was quite keen and bright but I can recall the Catholic school as inhibiting. My first real experience of racism by the teachers was at Christmas time. I went to the Christmas party and won a competition, the prize was a beautiful doll. I was told by a teacher that I had won the doll and was really pleased. I then saw a group of people, some teachers, looking at me and going into a huddle. Later, one of the ladies told me that I had not really won the doll, they gave me a little artificial Christmas tree instead. I never told my mum of the incident as she was so happy for me as I won a prize. That was a traumatic experience even at six years of age. I can see it plainly now and feel that was my first experience of racism. I was a questioning child at school and used to have lots of hassles with the teachers. They used to say 'well in your country' and sing bits of 'Way Down Upon the Swanee River'. Everybody in the class would turn around and look at me. Whenever I went to the gym they would ask me, are you Black all over, did you have a tail? and so on. Precisely what a lot of Black women are experiencing today. I had to resist people invading my privacy. Because of all that was happening to me I learnt how to fight. That was easy because my father treated me like a boy. He was disappointed I was not a boy as Africans like their first born to be a boy.

When I was eleven my school was preparing us for the scholarship to go to the convent. At that time things were really bad, shipping was contracting, and this affected my father who was a seaman. My mother who was a tailoress found that there was no work. For this scholarship I had four sittings. I had to pass the first and go on to the second and so on. I sat all four papers and felt proud of myself, though unlike the other kids I had no coaching at home. My father could hardly read or write in English and my mother was an ordinary working class woman who used to say to me 'don't waste your time reading'. My parents did not realise the value of reading, so I was on my own. After some weeks my mother went down to the education people to get the results. In those days most Black men who had White wives used to ask their wives to negotiate with housing, education and medical authorities etc. on their behalf. My mother found out that I had passed, but books, clothing, pencils etc. had to be paid for. The local authority paid the fees. The school I was to go to was a Catholic grammar school, but they later gave my place to somebody else because they said my parents could not afford it anyway. I was very very bitter, so bitter, but I would not cry. By this time I had built up a hate. I really hated White people, especially Catholics. For example, I would never let a teacher make me cry, even if it broke my heart. I would wait until I got to the toilet. What was unfortunate was that we were the only Black family in the area and neither my mother or father understood the education system, as a result they accepted what the system dished out to them. However, many families at that time did have their doubts about education, because they felt that schooling made their children look down on them. I am not sure whether this would have happened with my father or mother, but it was a case of a battle and my parents did not know how to fight it. I ended up in elementary state school being very anti-Catholic and later anti-religion. I remember reading a lot from early on and that gave me a good basis for school work. Generally, I was rejected at this stage in my schooling and refused to take part in many of its activities. I also got a kick out of reducing the teacher to tears. The teachers used to 'prime' the White kids against me and that made me more of a loner. There was only one teacher I could relate to. He was Mr Turner, the geography teacher, and geography was the only subject I was really good at. Mr Turner was able to tune into me and help me overcome my hostility and be able to cope with the school.

When I left school at fifteen, the thought of further education was not on. As far as my parents or I knew, no such thing existed. All I got from school was a testimonial (report) which was bad. I got absolutely

nothing from school after spending so much time there.
Things might have been better if I had not passed that
scholarship. I then would have accepted whatever I got.
However, with most of my schooling being Catholic, and I
hated them, it meant I had to work through my frustration.
In my experience open hostility comes to Black kids when
they get to eleven years of age. They are no longer
pickaninnies, they are actually becoming young men and
women, demanding things from the system like everybody
else, and as a result they are seen as a threat. In my
time at school I cannot remember any other Black kids
being there, though in Blackpool, there were some Irish
kids and a boy whose father was from Italy. He was darker
than you would think of people from Italy and the children
and teachers used to tease him and say to him that I was
his sister. I cannot say in truth that the school
prepared me for anything. There was no great motivation
by the teachers to help me in any way, except Mr Turner,
and I cannot remember any careers advice being given, but
I was now of working age. My dad had to help me get a
job. I often wonder how Black people survived in this
country in those days. Most of them wanted work but could
not get it, except during the war when they used anybody.
My father got a job in a plastic factory only because of
the war and labour was needed. While in that factory he
asked the boss if I could be an office junior, the boss
agreed and asked him to send me along. I was 5'5" and ten
stones. The boss perhaps expected a little girl with
pigtails. However, he did not give me a job although he
promised my father he would. I think my father was very
hurt and tried to protect me. I think he also realised
what a racist society Britain is. My father then told me
not to bother going out to work but to stay home with my
mother. At about that time we moved back to Manchester.
    I went job hunting when we came back to Manchester.
I used to go for jobs and be told how good the job was,
though very often you were asked to do many other things
than the advertised job stated. Many bosses made it clear
to me that their White workers would not want to share the
same toilet facilities with me. This was very humiliating
to me and the bosses did not want to upset his White work
force. My first job in Manchester was in a factory that
made clothes. While working there I was told by one of
the girls that after my interview Mr Blake, the boss,

called the work force together, about forty of them, and warned them all, that if any of them passed any remark or try to humiliate me they would be seriously dealt with. This was interesting because I worked there for six months before I knew that. While there, I really wanted to learn the tailoring trade but there were no opportunities. My horizons were very limited, maybe because there were no Black people to emulate, and I think that is very important. My father really wanted me to go into nursing, he was a very proud man, and felt that after my training I could go to Nigeria to practice my skills.

I got back into education much later in life. I had married with three children by then and on social security. I was also deeply involved in voluntary community work and the politics of Black people. You see, I was lucky to have a father who introduced me to politics as there were many Black people in this country who were politically confused, especially the light skinned ones. At this stage I decided to apply to the Polytechnic for a place on its youth and community course and, on acceptance and taking the course I found that I did not learn anything, as the course did not relate to what was actually happening to Black people. I had also done a number of W.E.A. courses especially on counselling, but also attended them to see what sort of material they were dishing out on race. I found the tutors knew very little of the issues concerning Blacks. Because of my experience, not my schooling, I am able to help my children and fight for them. I know that very often the schools are in the wrong, yet I see Black parents scold their children for things that happen at school. They blame the child. Very often my children were told by teachers to get back to your own country. Whenever this happened I used to go down to the school, challenge them, call them racist and picket the school. The school generally deals with stereotypes and they do not expect a Black person, especially a Black woman, to confront them. Very often they would speak to me over the phone and when I got down there they would be shocked, a Black woman with an English voice. I did not go into their world, I brought them into mine. They could never cope with that. They define Blacks as not intelligent - except the odd one or two - and they are surprised to meet an intelligent Black person.

I am not anti-White, but I am pro-Black. I am also very bitter, bitter for my children when racism takes place in schools. For example, an incident at my son's school. The school did the I.T.A. method of reading, and after some time with that scheme I was unhappy with his progress. I told him to ask his teacher to bring home some of the books and he told me that they did not allow that. I then made arrangements to see the headmaster. When I got there the head asked me into his office, and before I could say anything about my son the headmaster said 'it was too soon to find our whether your son was E.S.N.' Well!!! I got really mad and grabbed him by his collar, and maybe out of fright he collapsed. You see, what really got me mad was the head saying to me - though not his exact words - the child is Black, therefore it is very likely to be educationally sub-normal. It was complete stereotyping and I was not going to stand for it. Later I talked to the deputy head; apparently they did not have Black parents coming into the school to enquire of their children and I don't think a Black woman confronting their bureaucracy amused them.

The frightening thing was, if I was a woman who was not aware I would've doubted and blamed my own child and start treating him differently. To me it is extremely frightening because the word 'SPECIAL' as relating to school, is not what many people think it means. People, especially Black people, trust the school as they share the same values, though the rewards are different and that's where the conflict lies. When my daughter was at Central High School she told me that the teachers asked her to sing 'jumped on a Nigger's back and I thought it was a horse'. I told her to bring me the song and she did. I marched up to the school and was told by the headmistresss 'Do you expect us to exclude all our folk songs'. I said folk songs like that, yes. I said that as a Black woman I find them offensive. She said that she was not sure if she could do that, and I said, well, if it is not excluded I'll be out here picketing this school. They soon got rid of it, because they knew I would picket the school, because when my son experienced a similar situation at his school I picketed it. If you don't act they will trample over you. A number of Black kids get suspended from school without their parents being duly informed and often the parents accept this as they do not

understand the system and there's no one to advise them.
On another visit to Central High for a parents evening, I
saw an information plate on a desk which said 'IMMIGRANTS
TABLE'. I went straight across and demanded they got rid
of it. I said 'How dare you do that?' The head came up
to me and after some strong conversation they removed it.
You have to find ways of resisting racism.

     Education is one of the most damaging things because
of the way it is geared.   Even today with multi-
culturalism, they still look at us like 'them exotic
people' that need to be researched and looked at. Instead
of talking of multi-cultural they should be talking of an
anti-racist programme.   The multi-culture programme is
liberal and in itself is a kind of racism. The dominant
culture is the Black kids culture but because the rewards
are different we have uprisings in London, Bristol,
Liverpool and Manchester. In Britain institutional racism
is taking a greater foothold especially through the
introduction of legislation on Race and Health, the
Nationality Bill and so on, it is all fashioned to
perpetuate racism including the C.R.C. which has weakened
the position of Black people in this country.   It is
essential that the school relate its policies positively
to Black people, especially through subjects like
geography and history. Because of a lack of this view we
think totally European and this is a contributing factor
to the high percentage of Black people in mental homes,
the amount of Black kids up for adoption and the strained
situation existing between some Black kids and their
parents. The Black working class want to be White middle
class, not Black middle class. Again it is a matter of
lack of identification.

     In a sense adult education organised by the
authorities takes away the power of control and
participation from the community. This kills whatever is
going on, that is, spontaneous community response, and
secondly it keeps the information firmly in the hands of
white authority. This influence could be seen through
advice centres,child psychologists units, creches, E.S.N.
schools and so on. These agencies with others divert the
struggle, they duplicate everything and use their
resources to control Black people. We underestimate
racism in education. Do you know that I have evidence
which proves that some young Black people find it

difficult to accept a tutor who is Black? They will expect and accept someone White. What a society to be part of, eh?

Being rejected at school while so young was an important factor in understanding why at that stage she formed a distorted image of herself: an image which was to further influence her later participation in education. She had to cling to the warm and close relationship of her family, which was her only source of comfort, understanding and security. Unfortunately, her parents could not be as positive a force on her school life as she wished. Though interested, they had scant understanding of the education system. Her father could only communicate verbally in English, and her mother was a working class woman. Her mother, however, was the member of the family who negotiated with various social institutions on the family's behalf. This arrangement was not uncommon among symbiotic marriages at that time. Kath's success at school, therefore, depended on her own motivation.

Exam success and the loss of a place at school was a bitter experience.

No knowledge of the existence of post-school education.

Voluntary involvement with the black community, and the experience of a youth and community course.

CASE HISTORY 12 : RAPHAEL COLE

Born in England of an English mother (White) and a Nigerian father. Father had arrived in England in 1906; he was the youngest of twelve children. A seaman (so 'British' he had a tattoo of the Union Jack on his arm) on the Mauritania and Lusitania, as a stoker until the end of the first world war. During and after the second world war he worked as a scaler on the docks.

WHEN THE WAR was finished, Blacks on the docks were pushed out and their jobs given to Whites. My dad then got a job as a labourer in the gas works through a White friend. This friend, Mr Knowles, was a Communist and pushed for my dad. My dad was the only Black person employed there at the time though there were Blacks employed as labourers in the steelworks and wireworks in Liverpool. My father was very keen on schooling for us as kids, but when you ask me about education; education? Education for Blacks in this country is rubbish. It was in my time and now my children are going through it, it is still very poor. I'll tell you this, my nephew (sister's son) Sammy was sent back to Nigeria to be educated when he was eight years old. They sent him back because they felt that he would be better educated over there. When he came back to this country at twenty three and a chemist (pharmacist) he got a job in Boots, but left due to lack of opportunities. He went back to Nigeria where he now works for a large firm in Lagos. Out of all the children, grandchildren and great grandchildren born out of my parents, only Sammy did really well. I could remember in the 1940's when I started school there were two distinct and different groups, Blacks and Whites. It was a Catholic school which took us all through until we were fifteen years old. I remember when I was twelve Mr Murray took us for sports and for singing, I could see him on the piano now. One of the songs we used to sing was 'We came to the river and we couldn't get across, singing polly, wolly, doodle all the day. So we jumped on a nigger and he took us across, singing....' Mr Murray used to emphasise the nigger and turn to me and say 'there you are Colee, there's you.'

Sport? As far as football was concerned if you were as good as Pele he would not put you in the team. Cricket? No hope.

At fourteen and a half years old I could remember the priest Father Danny talking of the poor little black kids in Africa. I put my hand up and ask him what colour was God, he got very cross and said, 'We are not here for that, we are not here to discuss that'. He never spoke to me from that day, but he was like most of the teachers in that school. I only ever met one good teacher in that school. Irish, with ginger hair. I was still fourteen and a half and cock of the school because of my ability to defend myself. This Irish teacher called me and ask me why I'd hit this other lad, and I said, it was because he called me nigger. He, the teacher, said let me give you some advice 'if anyone ever calls you nigger ignore them because if they see that they hurt you, they'll call you all the more, and you will be the one who will be punished'. I could not take this any further, especially to my parents as they believed the teachers. Anyway, it

was three or four months before leaving school, and I
wanted a good report. My parents did not understand the
education system as they were only half educated
themselves. They could not really help us even though
they were interested. School, and memories of it isn't
nice. I could remember a lot of young teachers talking
about massacring Arabs. They weren't very nice people.
I've had my elder sister wanting to beat the teachers up
for calling us kids nigger. One day a teacher punched me
in the face. I thought I daren't go home and tell, but
somebody told my mom. She went down to school but the
headmaster talked her round. I remember the kids shouting
hey! Colee your mother is here to give Mr Moore (the
teacher) a good hiding.

Education in our day was lousy, it was not for us.
If you were bright and white it was O.K.but if you were
Black, no way. I'm not being funny but this is true. My
parents really thought that going to a White school in a
White country will be O.K. They'd never believe
otherwise. The education I got was nil. What hurts me
now at forty eight is not remembering but I have to spend
money on my children's education and they are getting a
second class education for it. Not only us but some of
the poor Whites too. I pay my rates and taxes etc. but if
I haven't got money to buy a good education for my kids I
can't get it. They go to second class schools which keep
the Black and White working class people in line. This
education system is made for people who have a natural
gift to learn despite the system and who have parents who
understand the system. But to say like we did, that going
to parents evening, making sure that they knew the three
'R's and to protect them against aggravation, is not
enough. Unfortunately we did not look at education as
having to pay for a good one, otherwise we would have. We
looked at home life, material things which we did not have
as kids. This is where we, the missus and I made a
mistake.

All I got from my ten years at St. Bernards R.C.
School was a letter, a testimonial to say I had attended.
That should have taught me a lesson. We had no exams or
things like that, the useless bit of paper was the only
proof of my education. When I finished there was not even
information on apprenticeship or careers. Most of what
was said on the reference was half lies and a load of

rubbish. The headmaster said of me 'My relationship with Philip Cole was agreeable, etc.' That was a lie, he was particularly racist in school. Mind you, my reference was a good one compared with what some of the other lads got. One of the Black lads, a fellow called Johnson taught himself to be a spark (electrician). He learnt the stuff from books and found a tradesman to go with. Another of my friends did the same in carpentry. I went into the clothing trade. In my age group out of twenty five leaving school only about three got jobs. All I was told when I left school by the priest was that on no condition must I marry a Protestant, he then gave me my testimonial.

The majority of Blacks in Liverpool got 'knocked back' that much they gave up. You don't see any Black faces in the large firms in Liverpool, you don't see them as teachers in schools, and you don't see them in Liverpool or Everton football teams. Yet Blacks have been in Liverpool for hundreds of years. The place is incredibly racist. My first job was in the rag trade at Quemby and Simpson. I started as a messenger and learnt to be a cutter and presser, and I got that job for myself; though I was surprised to get this job in such a posh shop. To get this job I had to wait outside St Thomas employment bureau and got a card off a bloke, who got a couple for himself, because they did not give Blacks cards for such jobs. This card had to be presented to the employer, and there's no surety you'll get the job. The employers asked me how I got the card, could I read, spell, count and so on. They also asked me what school I went to as some firms would not take Catholics. So before I go for a job I had to find out what sort of firm it was and get ready to lie. This was common practice.

At eighteen I had to go in the army for two years. I was determined not to join because of the hatred I had built up. The Mau Mau troubles in Kenya was going on, and some of the lads were sent out there. Some joined the army and would not go to Kenya as their fathers came from there, they were sent to Germany. To get away from the army I went to sea as a galley boy. This meant giving up my training as a cutter/presser, but is also meant getting a reference so that I could get on to a crash course for galley training. It was difficult for Blacks to get such letters and I went to all the shipping companies around Liverpool to get a letter to say that they would take me on after my six weeks training. After really hustling I got a letter off Lamport and Alt, which meant I could not go on any other line after my training. After my training I met yet another problem. Problems from the unions. They are against Black people. In the end I got in and went to sea. While I was at sea - over two years - I applied for second steward's posts and was always turned down. A couple of White lads who were on the course with me got promoted, and when I contested this they told me there were no more posts. P left and went back into the rag trade. I was about twenty years old then. The next big event was getting married, I was then twenty five.

I learnt my trade in Liverpool as the only other places to learn the trade were London and Manchester. I later moved to Manchester to practice my trade and was surprised that it was not as prejudiced as Liverpool. Liverpool must be the most racist city in this country. When you think, it was built on slavery. It is a major seaport and all sorts come through and this has been going on for hundreds of years. I've said before, you have to be born Black in Liverpool, grow up there, work there; to sit down and understand it, and talk about it. West Indians, Africans, any Black person who comes to Liverpool as an adult would experience racism, but being born there, going through the school system you realise what its like.

As a Black lad I went to school at Our Lady of Lourdes and St. Bernards and could not even serve mass in our local church. As Blacks we had to go down to Chinatown in a broken down shop. The front was knocked out and sheets put in. They would not even allow us to say mass in our own local church, be an altar boy or marry there. They even had a Catholic coloured mission, different from where the Whites used to go. That's religion for you. My brother-in-law at twenty three, a born Catholic, did his national service, was refused permission to marry in our local church. It was only because a hell of a fuss was kicked up and protests were made that permission was granted. This racism was everywhere, for example I can't remember seeing any Blacks in the University other than those who came from abroad. Not Liverpool born and bred, at least not in my day. Schooling today is only one step up from my time. Today they've got recreation halls, canteens and so on but the education they give is still much the same. My eldest daughter, now twenty two, went on to further education to take a catering course, she's got a good job and is engaged to be married. My youngest daughter is also in further education taking a secretarial course, but hoping to go into teaching later on. Both experienced a lot of racism in school and had to force their way through. My lad, the youngest, fifteen, is still at school and is hoping to go on to further education to do ''O' and 'A' levels. I remember my surprise when my daughter told me that there was a Black lecturer in her college. The best teachers in secondary seem to be in the Grammar school, and it helps if any parent has the cash to give their kid the extra help to pass the eleven-plus. The teachers in the secondary modern school are like those who taught us, and my kids had to have them. In my day it was difficult for Blacks and Catholics to get jobs disregarding your ability or skill, and employers used this to refuse us. Today I tell my children even though the law has been changed there are still loopholes employers will use, and impress on them the importance of doing well in education, especially Black people.

It is interesting to look back. My sisters' education was the same, except it was worse for them when they left school. They had very little to go on to other than machining or scrubbing and cleaning other people's houses. Nothing for any of us in Liverpool. It is a terrible shocking place to be born Black in. The things that happened during the recent riots, especially the behaviour of the police is nothing new. People seem surprised when I tell them that. It is a different generation but the experience is the same. The police with their alsation dogs used to shout at us 'C'mon coon, move'. They used to call the south end of Liverpool the jungle. It's now called Liverpool 8 or Toxteth. I always give the police a wide berth, I have seen too much. They are the true result of the education system, repressive and ignorant.

His parents did not understand the education system. However, they fully trusted it.

His schooling a very bitter experience.

The hostile attitude and behaviour of the police is nothing new.

CASE HISTORY 13 : MR. W.

Born in Liverpool, England. Mother English (White). Father from Sierra Leone. On arrival in England, his father could not read nor write in English.

THE PARTICULAR PRIMARY school I went to, took kids at three or four as the school had a nursery attached. The school (Harrington Board School) was located near the docks where many Black families lived, popularly known as Toxteth. In that school I was always top of the class, and I remember the teacher used to talk about this thing called 'the scholarship', and that I might pass it. Honestly my vision of scholarship was of some sort of a ship. I really had no idea, nor did my parents. The school had mainly White kids and a small number of Black kids. I was not too aware of racism in terms of different treatment from the teachers, but I remember the White kids calling us. We, the Blacks, were tough, so we did not get too much trouble anyway. We had exams every year, and at exam time I always finished second to a White guy called Kenny. Ron, another White guy was always third. At ten years of age most of my mates left Harrington and went to Granby Street school. The area I lived in was on the boundary of Liverpool 8, (Toxteth) where the majority of residents were White, and their kids went to Harrington. The school most Blacks went to was St. James's which was about two miles from where I lived. I asked, and my mom allowed me to go to Granby Street from Harrington to be with my mates. I struggled the first year at Granby Street and failed my eleven plus. Ron and Kenny who stayed at Harrington passed then went on to Toxteth Technical College. I would have passed had I stayed on at Harrington and my life might be different. In fact Harrington had a good record of putting kids through eleven plus. Naivety you know, not only on my part but also on my parents side, in that they allowed me to leave Harrington. I will always remember the teacher saying 'You've got a good chance for your scholarship, don't you leave now and spoil your chances'. This scholarship business seemed miles away, somewhere in the sky.

While in the first year at Granby Street, I remember going home worried for the first time in my life. I could not do the maths. I later got into my stride and between the age of eleven to fourteen I finished top of my class at Granby Street. I took the thirteen plus while there and to this day I do not know how I failed, because I finished that well in advance, that I thought, 'Well, I've passed this'. People well down the class passed and I failed. The only reason I could think for failing was that I must have turned two pages in one go and missed some questions? I just don't know. I stayed on at Granby Street till I was fifteen. The turning point in my education was at that time, Liverpool Education Board tried out this special experiment for three or four years. What they did was to take kids from secondary school, at fifteen, and give them an extra year at a technical school - West Derby Secondary Tech. This was a unique experiment at that time and designed to give a year's technical education to enable kids to compete for apprenticeships in engineering. I was the only one from our school who took it and passed. While at Granby Street I became head boy and school captain (football) and regularly finished top of the class, yet I did not know what a G.C.E. was. We took no exam whatsoever, other than for this special experiment. When we left school all I got was a testimonial and that was the end of it. That was in 1957-1958. Granby Street was a tough, tough school. I have since learnt that many of the teachers who taught us came straight out of training college and stayed only a short period before moving on to a safer post.

Going to West Derby Tech. opened my eyes. There were two other Black kids, which surprised me; we had to wear full uniform and the masters wore gowns. In a sense it was an interesting experience. I was always well behaved at school, being head boy and that. I loved, loved school especially in the very early years. There was a difference however when I went to West Derby, there were lots of things I had never done. Classes were made up of kids from all over Liverpool and I found in maths, for example, I was way behind. I could not do half the stuff the other kids did and they used to laugh at me. I got my head down and finally got to about the middle of the group. At the end of the first year I finished about eleventh out of about thirty. Interesting enough I changed in other ways while at West Derby. I turned out to be a baddie. For some reason our class was regarded as the 'divis', (not very bright). I went along with that and it got me into trouble. I had no racial problems that I could not deal with, in a sense that was my salvation. I was the only Black person in my class, though there were two younger Black guys in other classes in the school. West Derby was also different in other respects to Granby Street. At Granby Street there were no careers guidance to speak of. All the kids got jobs as van boys or work in stores. Dead end jobs. In Derby Tech. there was a proper careers teacher and list of firms to write to for apprenticeship. I learnt from this situation how to get into a trade. I wrote to about twenty firms, got one interview and got an apprenticeship. The firm was English Electric, and the apprenticeship was in engineering. After getting this apprenticeship I was called for interviews with Manweb and Gas Board. I decided to stay at English Electric and was part of a very structured system. I went to the company training school and was allowed one day a week to go to college, where I did my

O.N.C.   In those days it was the S1, S2 and S3, S3 being the final for the O.N.C.   A lot of kids went for City and Guilds but I wanted the O.N.C.   I struggled through the first and second year of O.N.C. work and passed.   Come the third year, my final, I failed.   I was nineteen then and failing meant that the firm would not pay for repeats, and it also meant the end of day release and the beginning of night school.

At that time I was heavily involved in playing football but with a mate of mine, Eddie, a White guy. I applied for day school.   Eddie had also failed, and was on the night shift so it was possible for him to attend day school.   I was on day shift, but also went along to day school, at the end of the first term the education officer called me in and said, 'you failed last year?'   I said yes, sir.   He said 'you can't go to day school'.   I explained that I trained for football two nights a week. He said, 'you know the rules, you can't go to day school'. I said stop my pay, he said 'no, you are employed here five days a week, go to night school'.   So I had to go to night school.   Eddie who went to day school passed and went on to get his H.N.C.   The last time I saw him he was into management of a factory.   I found night school difficult, especially being tied up with football training, and could not cope with it.   I gave up the idea of studying.   I stayed in engineering for sixteen years, served my time, got some experience of office work, did a bit of work study aand spent some time in the draughtsman's section.   I did a bit of everything.   I was also a part-time professional footballer.   Football was my life.   I was also a shop steward and attended the relevant courses through the union.   As my football career came to an end I got involved in voluntary youth work (part-time) and was later offered a full-time job at a youth centre.   Though I had a good job in engineering I had always fancied social work.   This youth project was funded through the Gulbenkian foundation, so my salary was comparable to what I got in engineering.   I was also promised social work training.   After three years as a youth worker I was seconded to the Polytechnic to take the Youth and Community course.   I loved it, and passed well.

Having finished there I got involved with the educational aspects of youth work.   I was interested in trying to bridge the gap between the school situation, the college scene and youth work. The informal and the formal. I then set up a project in an attempt to bridge the gap. I also wanted to further my studies, to do further training. I applied to University to take the Diploma in Adult Education and was refused because I did not have a first degree, and not being a teacher I was not allowed on the course. I contacted a tutor in the Education department (adult) and he told me he would put my case to the faculty board. I was later asked to produce some evidence of my ability to cope with the course, and was told that my evidence will be considered. I wrote a lengthy piece arguing my case, and was accepted as a visiting student. This meant participating in a sort of pre-Diploma course. I did this for the year and my performance was deemed satisfactory. The department agreed to take me on the Dip. A.E. Course, which I successfully completed. I am now back into community work full-time and will give myself two to three years and then consider further study, perhaps the M. Ed. in Youth and Community. While at the University everything went really smoothly, and I would like to think that I contributed something. In this particular University Department there were many Black students, though they were in the main from overseas. Racism did not seem to exist, or perhaps its more open at schools. I remember the Christmas pantos at school. This particular year they chose this Black boy to play the part of a lazy person lying in the sunshine and sung 'Lazybones'. We also did something about the river Niger in Africa and I got this thing to read with the word 'nigger'. I said I would not read it, and the teacher said it had to do with the river, but I still refused. Other than such incidents I could not say that there was much racism. I had little trouble in my school career. The reason for this was that I was a popular person, and I was good at football. On the odd occasion when anyone called me my mates dealt with them.

When I left school and went into semi-pro football there was much more open racism from both players on the opposing teams and their supporters. Again it was always my mates (White) who reacted quicker than me. So that never really bothered me, there is a lot of racism in football. The city of Liverpool the best example. Racism at work came as a different kind of experience. English Electric was on the outskirts of Liverpool about seven miles from where I lived and away from the Black community. The factory had a workforce of about 12,000 people of which five were Blacks. I was the only Black apprentice for the sixteen years I was there. The other Black lads were labourers. I remember the White lads feeling my hair because they've never been with a Black person before. In the north of Liverpool you did not see many Black people. In the factory I went about my business and never got into any major hassles. I played a low profile. As apprentices we all sat together to work and for breaks, the only division was according to year of apprenticeship. During the tea-breaks we would all tell jokes, sometimes they would say, hey' you know we've seen niggers walking down the road, then they would check and say Oh! sorry mate. At that time I did not respond, but if the same or similar statements are made today I'll just tell the person to cut that out.

I became a shop steward because I knew my job, I played semi-pro football and was well liked. I frequently had my name in the weekend paper and was a goal scorer. As you know the people of Liverpool love their football. The factory was football mad. I was also a caring union organiser and representative and felt that people could relate to me. Because of my colour, experience and problems over the years I was very sensitive to people, but took everybody as an individual. As the union rep I had to deal with out-of-work situations, problems with rent and so on, and I got a reputation for helping people. I went from the shop floor into the office as a union rep for ASTMS and was the senior negotiator amongst three for the whole factory. The other two were the foreman and the works superintendent. I had no problem relating with anyone on the negotiating panel. You must remember I was born in England, English. Hear my accent? I am a scouser. In those days however, I had more to do with the White community than the Black. I was an Englishman with a black face, very unconscious about Black issues as I lived and worked outside the Black community. At work I did get reports back about people saying that they had a nigger as a negotiator, bleeding wogs. I understood the workers would always say, 'We don't care what colour he is if he does the job he's O.K'. Management also reacted to me quite well. I remember we had a strike and had to sort out some problems of 'cowboys' trying to deliver to the firm. When the strike was over my boss called me in the office and said, 'Who do you think you are?' I said 'What do you mean?'. He then said 'You are management, on salary review, yet you are on bloody strike telling people not to pick up stuff from the factory, you are pushing your luck'. I said as a union representative I was within my rights to influence the situation. 'You smart bastard' he said and that was the end of it.

The reason I did not do better in education especially at an early age was to some extent due to my father. He was very strict and insisted that I got a trade. When I passed my exam at fifteen my dad was made up (delighted). I remember he took me for a drink when he went down to the pub. The ship's chief engineer was in the pub; my dad proudly told him of my exam success, though my dad was unable to give me real advice on education or career, except to get a skill. He did not want me to be a boiler scaler as he was.

In real terms, I don't think colour has ever held me back, though sport helped a lot. My situation has all been chance as most of the lads I left school with got in trouble with the police. I think my learning came not in the school, but in adult educatin and the factory. The factory world brought me out and showed me other things, like how to negotiate, how to handle racism and so on. I learnt the power of words in adult education. Mind you, for sixteen years I had no notion of the Black experience. I was thirty before I became really politically conscious about Black issues. The last ten years has been a learning period for me, a real learning period about the Black community. It's made me think, 'What have I been doing with my life?' If I had this consciousness when I was younger it would have been different. My father was passive and as a result did not pass on to me a need to be inquisitive and proud of my race. As a teenager all my mates were White, though when we went to dances I was rejected. I frequently made excuses for my situation, until the day when I made excuses to them and opted to go back into the Black community.

Getting involved in voluntary part-time work in the Black community was a useful way of neutralising this disappointment. The part-time commitment was later converted to full time participation, and opened the door to adult education. Gaining a qualification was important to Mr. W. but fulfilment and learning assumed greater importance. Being involved in the community and in Adult Education have given Mr. W. an opportunity to reflect on the importance of education to him. A single telling response is that he felt cheated. While making many gains through education, the lack of a knowledge and consciousness of his identity, the nature of the society he lived in, the lack of direction and fulfilment at school, is all part of Mr. W's regret about the school system. He is however very supportive of adult education. To him it is the most beneficial sector of education in this country and we are fortunate in having a second chance.

Passed fourteen plus for place at technical school - a turning point in Mr. W's life. Tech school a more formal system of education and preferred by Mr. W.

Overt racism not a significant feature of school life. Though Mr. W's change in attitude is attributed to his response to covert racism.

His feeling of Englishness a superior factor in his life.

Rejection by his White peers triggered the notion of Black consciousness for Mr. W. This made for a changed view of his life situation.

CASE HISTORY 14 : ARTHUR JACKSON

Born in Jamaica, Mr Jackson completed his schooling, apprenticeship and initial work experience in that country. He decided to emigrate to England in response to the request by the British Government for a communal effort during the second world war. He also wanted to further his education.

I **LEFT SCHOOL** at fifteen and went into a motor coach building apprenticeship. I had to leave school due to the lack of money in the family. What money my parents had went on my eldest sister who was doing well at school. This apprenticeship was cut short as orders for coach bodies fell. With my uncle's help I was able to get another apprenticeship. This time in a large firm of engineers and founders. This apprenticeship did not include any off-the-job schooling as the firm did not approve. If any of the apprentices wanted to go to night school, they had to hide that fact. My only off-the-job learning during this period, came from books given to me by a friend. I also wrote to Bennett College of England to enrol for their correspondence course in diesel engineering. Before that information arrived I had to leave Jamaica for England. The second world war had started, and all over Jamaica there were posters asking young men to volunteer to help the mother country in her time of need. Also, there was little room for personal progress in Jamaica, plus the fact that political strife was brewing. Many people felt trapped. Being loyal subjects the young lads were eager to get to England to do their bit. Those who were too old, sadly wished that they were young enough to fight for King and country. Britain especially needed people with engineering skills as most of her native engineers had gone to war. I was then at the journeyman stage so I volunteered. Our ship docked in Greenock, Scotland after the most hazardous trip I have ever been on.

During the war, ships had to travel in convoy up to Canada from the West Indies; then to Greenland, so as to avoid German U-boats. Both the weather and the U-boats took their toll however, and many of our lads were lost. In one case a group of fifty lads from Barbados were reduced to five. They were torpedoed several times, and those who survived never got over the shock. Looking back now, I think of the loyalty we had for England. We would have done anything for her. Sadly, I no longer have this feeling for her after my experiences in this country. I arrived in Manchester from Scotland and was sent to the government training centre for three months. After that period I was sent to Metropolitan Vickers for a further three months. Having completed this industrial acclimatisation, I was surprised to learn that the trade union would not have us as members. The union had two ways of identifying its work people. Members had a green card and they were for the Whites. Blacks were given brown cards which meant that we Blacks had what they called 'dilutee' status. We were seen as diluting the pure skill of the white man. The fact that I and my Black mates in the trade were all skilled meant nothing. Any skills acquired outside the six weeks acclimatisation were unacceptable. To obtain a green card we, the Blacks, had to serve five years, and get an experienced engineer to sponsor us. That wasn't easy. In fact the whole situation was very frustrating.

In any case, I continued a draughtsman course I had started with the British Institute of Engineering Technology. I also passed an entrance exam allowing me to attend college on Sunday, as evening classes had ceased. These courses were at the Manchester College of Technology, now U.M.I.S.T. There were not many Blacks on the course, and I found that attending part-time classes, taking a correspondence course and earning a living was too much. I dropped the correspondence course and continued at college. It took me the required six years to get my O.N.C., H.N.C. and Associateship of the Institute. On completion I applied to take a course in Civil Engineering, but found that this was only accepted if I worked for the local authority. At least that is what they told me. I had no way of finding out if this was true as careers advice centres did not exist then. I however, knew that it was impossible as a Black man, to find employment in local authority offices. I was knocking on doors that were closed to me and I did not know this. The only Blacks seen in government offices were those from overseas, who were being trained to go back and administrate in their own country. I also soon found out that being fully qualified made no difference in terms of occupation. I wrote off for dozens of jobs, but was never offered one to match my skills and qualifications. I was even subjected to training White lads, who were then put over me. That sort of thing hurt me a lot, but what could I do? I also knew of teachers at the Tech who were teaching just below the year they were studying, and were less qualified and experienced than me. I was not even considered for that sort of job.

I was out of work and desperate for a job. I was going for everything and anything. Through an advertisement in the papers, I applied for a work-study engineer's job at Metro Vicks. I got through the first and second interview, and was told by the personnel manager that I was just the person for the job. He then added that he could not offer me the post as I worked on the shop floor before, and the men there will not accept me in such a senior position.

If race is the reason for my lack of job promotion, it is not that the employer objected to me. The employer has a product to make, a job to do. He wants it done as efficiently, as cheaply, and as good as he could get it done. The employer is afraid that he may lose a client, or that there will be disturbance on the shop floor, if he employs me. The employer feels that a Black man will not be able to control a group of Englishmen. The boss does not agree with these views, but what can he do? He can't afford to disrupt his factory. A lot of us, Black people, shout about colour prejudice, but we haven't looked at the poor blokes who have a factory to run.

I also applied for a job at Reynolds Chains; a Dutch firm with a branch in Manchester. The personnel manager tried all manner of means not to give me that job. I suspect he did not expect me to be coloured, as my name and qualifications might not have suggested that. First he said the union would not accept me: and was surprised when I showed him my union card. He then said 'Oh! I see you've served your time'. He should've known that, as this information was on my application form. He then paused and said, 'I think the job will not suit you as you are over qualified for it'. I was a bit fed up with the situation, but was not too surprised. I knew of African lads with Masters degrees working on the docks as labourers. In fact, Blacks only started to get a few good jobs with the formation of C.A.R.D. The Campaign Against Racial Discrimination. This organisation was formed in 1958-1959. There was a crying need for such an organisation, as none existed then, and before, to help Blacks resident in this country, with the support of a number of White liberals; including the daughter of Sir Stafford Cripps. The organisation also gained media support, though only from the Manchester Guardian. An interesting point, in that the Guardian was also the only paper to report the deliberations of the Pan-African Conference. The efforts to get coloured people a better deal even goes back before Pan-Africanism. Before the war there was an organisation called the Ethiopian Brotherhood whose main platform was anti-colonialism. When the war started they were banned and that meant they could not officially take part in the Pan-African Conference. Together these groups did a lot for coloured people, but C.A.R.D. did most for those who worked and lived in the United Kingdom.

There was also a lot of aggravation in the social

life of Black people then.   Many Black men married White
women as there were few Black women about.   This caused a
lot of strife amongst White men and influenced the
government to encourage Black men to bring their wives
over to England.   There was now a new generation with
parents from different racial groups.   Sometimes the guy
would be White and his wife Black, but more often it would
be the other way round.   These children had to face
another sort of problem in school.   For my own part,
whatever prejudice my children felt, was never fed back to
me.   I knew they could come up against it, especially my
daughter.   She was the eldest and very sensitive.   I said
to her she should not make herself conspicuous at school
in any way.   She should lie low, and absorb what was being
taught.   I felt that if she made herself too conspicuous
they would turn her out.   You see, in my time at college,
I asked questions but did not go to any extreme in being
obvious.   I did not even socialise much out of class.   My
daughter understood and was very successful.   After a
Grammar education, she went to University to study
Economics.   She got a good degree and is now working in
education.   My eldest son was given the same advice, won a
place at Grammar school and a scholarship at Cambridge.
He studied Medicine there and is now working in the West
Indies.   My second son obtained his degree in Metallurgy.
My third son is in computers and my youngest daughter is
still at secondary school.

My wife and me believe that to surmount prejudice
Black people must get through the education barriers.
This has been the driving force for our children.   We also
joined the Parent Teacher Association and were active
members.   I think what prejudice they experienced came
from the playing fields, not from the teachers.   Though, I
remember at the time of Sharpeville, an incident with the
headmaster of my eldest lads' school.   He stood up in
front of the school, at assembly, and said: if he had his
way he would shoot everyone of those Blacks down.   My son
has not forgotten and never forgave him for saying that.
This same headmaster, however, did everything possible to
help him.   What is never quite clear to Blacks in England
is that they see a collective English attitude to them.
Individually, Blacks can have great friends with Whites,
as I have.   They look at me like most Whites look at their
Black friends: as being different.   They have taken me out

of the lot and see me differently. They, the Whites, are collectively racist, but not necessarily so individually. For example, take the school. When a teacher takes a dislike to a Black child, it is no use complaining because the headmaster will support his staff. The teacher can then make the child suffer, and I have seen this happen. The education system is not geared to change prejudice. The system is loaded with contradictions, and very often disregards our contributions.

I have had an opportunity to be educated at a high level, and achieved recognised qualifications. This however has made no difference to my promotion prospects. Although I have, through my employment history in the U.K., had high praise from all my employers. I have never been promoted above any of my fellow workmates who are White. I have not even moved into what would appear to all as a better post. Any movement up came from changing jobs, or waiting until my seniors in position moved to a new post, left the job, or died.

I still believe the education system can change things, though I do not agree in positive discrimination and multicultural education as I understand it. Positive discrimination is lowering the education standards. The needs of Blacks is the same as Whites as education is not built on race. What happens is the system is modified by some people to show the Whites as superior. If you remove that modification then you have education as it should be, and no need for multiculturalism or positive discrimination. It is this bias education system that has alienated young Blacks as issues like the race riots show. We, the old ones used to think that when the Black kids, born in this country grow up it will be all right, but this is not the case. Laws like they have in America won't help so it is up to teachers and parents to make things change. The onus for change however is with the Blacks themselves.

The journey and settling in England led to much disappointment and sadness with life in Britain.

He was further disappointed at finding a high level of racism in the workplace.

Racism in schools was not part of his children's experience, according to him.

CASE HISTORY 15 : MRS JACKSON

A housewife, White, born and educated in England.

I HAVE ALWAYS been at home when the children arrived from school, I participate actively in the P.T.A. and never stepped back if anything happened at school that I was not pleased with. I go to the school and tackle it. I have introduced all my children to the library at an early age and always tried to keep them in advance of school work. To do this we often bought them advance copies of the books they were going to use. We also see it as our duty to tell them about the exams they are going in for, never made it sound like the end of the world attempt, and never gave them private tuition. The private lessons issue was partly because we could not afford it.

We always restricted their television watching, and encouraged them to take up a musical instrument. The eldest boy is a good musician, he plays the clarinet. The eldest girl plays the piano and the youngest the clarinet.

The second boy plays the violin and the third boy the saxophone. The eldest boy and girl were influenced by us, but they influenced their younger brothers and sister. The motivation for school work came from my husband. He's always worked and studied hard, and the eldest kids remember him working night after night on his college work. I found that the eldest girl helped the eldest boy in his school work, though both of them took longer to read than the middle boy. The middle boy read through memory and the youngest boy, an early starter, actually started to read for himself. The younger three realised the success of the elder two and wanted to do as well, especially the second boy, who is the third child.

With regards career choice, the eldest girl decided for herself with the help of her teacher, who turned out to be her great friend. The eldest boy decided he wanted to be a doctor from very young. We are not quite sure how this came about and think that it may be from visits I had from the doctor when the second son was not too well. The second son's career was influenced by people at the firm who employed him during his school holidays. The firm dealt with developments in plastics and so on, and he decided that was what he wanted to study. The third son's interest in electronics developed from an interest in school. As yet we are not sure what the youngest will do but there's lots of time yet. The proudest day in our lives was when my eldest daughter won a scholarship to Grammar. This was especially significant because of all the bother we had with her primary and junior schooling. The headmaster seemed to accept the view that none of the children in the school would have done well. Incidentally, the same thing happened with the eldest boy in the same school; but he had the experience of his sister to go by.

I was very protective to the eldest girl. I could not be sure she would not be molested, so I always took her to and from school. With the rest of the family it was different, they were boys and were more confident. An important part of our family life is that we always took them to the theatre, especially Gilbert and Sullivan productions. Also, we always holidayed together, even if it was just a cycling holiday.

She   introduced them to the library in their pre-school years and bought copies of books they were about to use in school.

She participated actively in the P.T.A.

She gladly accepted the role of the link between home and school, as her husband was working and studying. Like her, he actively participated in the P.T.A. but often she took the lead. Both felt it was necessary to be single minded about education and decided to forgo other things to make sure the children did well at school. Over the years Mrs Jackson noticed the difference between the children's views, especially the boys,and their father's. The boys became very political and were not prepared to accept racism. Their father on the other hand could not bring himself to believe that his lack of opportunities and progress was due to racism. For her own part Mrs Jackson accepts that racism was the central feature in her husband's experience, and is quick to praise and admire his determination and absence of hate. She was however too modest to claim that her family's achievement was anything special.

CASE HISTORY 16 : CHARLES GLOVER

Aged twenty, Charles was born and educated in England. His parents are Jamaican and both are employed in the state transport industry. A Rastafarian, Charles received some training as a painter and decorator but is presently unemployed.

I **CAN'T REMEMBER** anything significant about my primary school, except we had no exams to decide which school to go on to. In fact the only alternative was the E.S.N. school. All the kids from our area went to the same primary and secondary school. I was always a 'baddie' in secondary school, always in trouble. Some teachers showed an interest in me, but I did not pay much notice. I remember one particular Black teacher who was really interested in helping me. He was strict and I felt that I got on better with teachers who were strict. Some pupils may not like them, but they get things done. With this particular teacher I did as I was told whether at school or for homework.

In the schools I went to there were kids from different races. I got on great with any of them I met. I had no problems with White kids; in fact they wanted to get in with me because I was seen as the 'hard guy' in school. The black kids was different, they used to challenge my position. The relationships in the school yard did not really interfere with my class work, though I did not do much in class. I was told by more than one teacher that I had it in me to do well, but I must give up some of my friends as they are a bad influence. I was also very involved in sport and was captain of the school football team. This involvement in sport had more effect on my class work than fighting in the yard. In the first two years at secondary we did not get any exams. What we did get was a set of questions, all with the same pattern and no relevance to anything. No intelligence was needed to answer them, I just had to use my imagination.

In the third year I chose to do English, maths, history, art and tech drawing; even though I was hopeless at tech drawing. We did not do any science subjects at all, but we did do gardening. I did not enjoy history lessons or get anything from it. The teacher was not interested at all, she used to come into the class, give the books out, told us to read and carried on doing something else. When she did talk to us it was all about the White man who discovered this and that. I suppose it all went in one ear and out the other. I found maths hard, but really enjoyed English and art. In the fourth year it was suggested that I may take C.S.E's but that came to nothing. At this time I had begun to become involved in the Rastafarian religion as it was the only thing that seemed to offer me anything. I went to school with my hair plaited, and all hell broke loose. The teacher said there was no way I was going to his class like that, but I went into school anyway. This teacher went to see my parents and that was when the pressure really started.

I felt it was my life and if I wanted to walk around like this, then they had to accept my wishes. They should judge me on what I could offer, what I have inside me, not on my appearance. In any case school did not have anything better to offer and all around me there were hypocrites and racists. I must admit though that I felt bad to let the Black teacher down. I think he wanted me to be a model for the younger ones. Anyway, my belief was important to me, and my hair was part of it. 'Dread' represented my belief in God and led me to read the Bible, even though the Bible said I did not have to be 'dread' to be a Rasta. 'Dread' to me is a covenant, a sign of my belief. This belief has nothing to do with the non-education they offering. The Bible deals with reality, it explains everything that is happening in the world today. I decided to quit school. In fact my final school report was not very bad, though it made no mention of me going dread. It is typical of the school, if I conformed it was O.K. If not, that's it. The school gave no real advice to me that was useful during the time I was there.

After leaving school I was involved in a fight and was accused of mugging which I did not do. My dread must have made it worse, I was arrested and sent to detention for six months. Six months for my first offence and I did not even do it. Detention was like a school, the only difference was that I could not go home. I had this tutor, a Scottish guy who wook an interest in me and tried to understand Rasta. The most interesting thing I did while there was to go on a painting and decorating course which lasted until I left. I got a credit for my efforts and was looking forward to making a career in that trade. I found when I came out that I could not get a job. Nobody was prepared to give me a chance. Not even the job-creation people. I went around for months and not a thing turned up. It was then I was involved in a second offence and was sent to Risley for one year on remand. The screws at Risley are all National Front people. No matter how polite I tried to be, they'd have a go at me. They called me nigger, coon and all the insults under the sun. They physically mistreated me and I didn't dare complain. Risley is lonely, cold and cruel. I could have died in that place. The screws gave me a really bad time. The people at Risley did not even offer any form of training. I was locked in my cell for most of the day except for meal times and exercise. I've been through a really bad time at that place. When I came out the police started giving me a hard time. Just walking in the street, they would stop me and harass me. I've been punched, framed and threatened. In fact, court records

will show that the police were guilty of framing me.   It
all started for something I did not do and my belief in
Rasta.   They call this a free country.   My father never
understood the whole scene, so he was not much help.   My
mom really tried.   She's my best friend and I really feel
sad about letting her down.

I am not too satisfied with the education and advice
that I've had, except for that one teacher's attempt.   The
majority of people want to keep me down.   If I was sure it
was my hair, my dread, that was stopping me from going
places I'll cut it.   But I did that once and didn't get
anywhere.   At school I had no advice on careers.   They
just sent me to the job centre where they blamed my hair
for my lack of success.   If the school taught me things
that was useful, I could see the point;   but I just got
bored.   It is easy to get bored in school.   The most
hurtful thing is that this is my country too.   Some Jews
have dread, hippies have long hair.   Both get chances, why
can't I?   Why can't I keep my identity and prosper at the
same time?

I don't see much hope for a change.   There's no point
going   back   to   education.   I   know   lads   who   have
qualifications and who haven't got dread;   and still they
haven't got a job.   There's no point.   Education did not
help me in the past and I certainly can't see it helping
me now.   What I've got to do is to read my Bible and keep
out of the police way.

Charles recounts his mother as making a determined effort
on his behalf but she believed in what the head and other
teachers had to say. His father, on the other hand did
not try to understand, mainly because Charles made no real
attempt to conform. Charles transferred his
dissatisfaction with schooling to post-school learning
activities and is not interested in further participation.
This view is strengthened by his known acquaintances who
hold different kinds of certificates, and are unemployed.

Meeting Charles was quite fortuitious and started with the
writer passing the time of day in a street encounter.
Charles was a bit surprised as he stated 'Even some black
people are hostile to me'. He enquired about the sorts of
things the writer did and enthusiastically volunteered to
participate. He later suggested that the writer talk to
other members of his family.

Strict teachers are more effective, though most of his showed a lack of interest.

Involvement with Rastafarianism.

No guidance from school.

'Labelled' by the police.

Not satisfied with the education he had.

CASE HISTORY 17 : CHRISTINE GLOVER

Born and educated in Jamaica, she passed the High School entrance exams (High school in Jamaica similar to Grammar in Britain) but was unable to take up that opportunity as she had to join her parents who were already resident in England. She trained as a secretary and is at present a mother and housewife.

A SHORT TIME after my arrival in England my parents took me to the further education college to enrol on a two year course in pre-nursing. The choice of course was really my mom's as she would have loved to be a nurse herself. Due to my lack of interest in nursing I requested and was granted a transfer to secretarial studies. Nursing seemed too easy and too many West Indian parents seem to push their daughters into nursing. Anyway, I wanted to do somthing different from the majority of Black girls.

At college I soon recognised some differences as compared with schooling back home. There, teachers are more strict, punishment - caning - is allowed, and school rules are more strictly enforced. I also became aware of racism, as in Jamaica I never thought of racial differences. Coming to think of it, I now realise it was there in a way; but I never really thought of it before facing it in this country. In Jamaica some Whites went to special school, e.g. boarding, while most of the other children on the island went to state school. Even though this situation existed there was not the level of tension you get in this country because of race. In further education college there were only four other Black girls in the group, and like me they were all from overseas. There were some Jewish girls too, and I got on really well with them; maybe because they are also from a minority group. I found that the teachers used to pick on the Black girls, though not me particularly. I don't know whether it was because they stood out or for not doing their work properly: but they were chastised more often than the White girls on the course. I am not saying that the teachers are prejudiced, but when a group is in the minority they stand out and often get blamed if anything goes wrong. Personally, I got on fairly well with the teachers and was awarded a prize for my efforts.

Unfortunately, while at college I received no careers advice and went to register at Brook Street Bureau. They were really helpful and soon found me a part-time post as a secretary at the Business School. My employers at the school found my work satisfactory and made my post full-time. When I started off at the Business School my employers invited my parents to have a look around the place I was to work. I thought that was really nice. They were very good employers and my race never came into it. While there I was also encouraged to take a modelling course by my immediate boss. She felt that I would do well as a model, though I did not do well as a model, but I did not think of it in terms of a full-time occupation. I found out while on the course there was a lot of racism in modelling. The fashion manufacturers' attitude is that there is a lot of prejudice among the buying public, especially people who buy through mail order. They feel that the general public may like an item but will be put off it, if they see it on a black person. The manufacturers will only use a black girl if she is famous, like Grace Jones . My only venture into further education was to take Spanish at evening classes. In Jamaica Spanish is the second language, as French is here. I also liked it as a language but did not take it with a job in mind.

After two and a half years at the Business School I wanted a change and saw an advert for girls who wanted to train as croupiers. It sounded very different and exciting, so I applied. I was surprised to be selected and was sent on a short course. This increased my awareness of the differences in people, and developed my confidence in myself. I found my employers pleasant to work with, though some of the customers and most of the girls I worked with were prejudiced. Though this really never bothered me, I left soon after as I was to be married and the long hours at the club was unsocial. After leaving the club I got a job as a secretary in an advertising agency, and soon found some of the staff, mainly the girls, resented my presence. They seemed surprised that a Black person could be educated. I was called names, and duly reported the incidents to my boss. He soon sorted it out and things got a little better. This attitude does not seem to be related only to work situations. I did not attend secondary school over here but I noticed my brother's and sister's work at school and listened to the things they had to say when they came home from school. It seems that some teachers did not push the Black kids. I have seen my brother's work books with grammatical errors left uncorrected. They also never seemed to have much work to do at home. I felt that some of the teachers weren't bothered. This lack of care seemed to rub-off on the students and make them think something was wrong with them. This will no doubt affect their confidence, especially when it comes to going and competing for jobs.

I was brought up in an environment where I was completely equal with everyone, other than the few Whites from overseas whose parents had top jobs. In such a situation my ability counted, not my colour. In England I have to hold on hard to that attitude; that I

am as good as the next person. A positive attitude. I
feel that if anyone grew up in a society where the
influence is negative the behaviour will be negative.
In Jamaica, no matter what your colour the teachers want
everyone to succeed.

The degree of racist intolerance in English society was a surprise to her.

The multi-cultural nature of further education was a positive influence in her participation in education.

The lack of carrers guidance at college was a dispiriting factor in planning her future.

CASE HISTORY 18 : PAULINE GLOVER

<u>PAULINE GLOVER</u>

Born and educated in England, Pauline is the second child and daughter, but the first in the family to experience all her education in England. She is employed in an administrative post with a mail order firm.

MY PRIMARY EDUCATION is a happy playful childhood memory. Academic work was not important in our school then as things at school weren't designed to send anyone to Grammar. Two things stand out in my memory of secondary education. One was the school's interest in getting Black kids to participate in sports, and secondly the lack of interest the teachers showed in 'pushing us'. We did not do 'O' levels, but took the C.S.E. exams. My subjects were English, Maths, Typing and Housecraft. I enjoyed English, but was no good at Maths. In any case I was looking forward to going out to work to earn some money, and school couldn't finish soon enough for me. Most of my friends wanted to do nursery nursing but I was not interested in that type of work. When we got into the fifth year the careers advice officer came around and asked us what we wanted to do when we left school. Also, the school wanted me to do nursery nursing but I was not interested in that type of work. When we got into the fifth year the careers advice officer came around and asked us what we wanted to do when we left school. Also, the school organised an introduction to work programme. Both ideas were interesting but in the end I still had to go out and find a job myself, without knowing much about all thatr might be available that I could do. I found a job myself with the help of a friend who knew of a vacancy in the place where she worked. To get this job I had to do a speed test and because of this I saw some use for the typing, English and Maths I did at school. The firm sent me on a training course organised by them and this gave me an opportunity to get some skills training which helped me to move on to another firm after a year.

Looking back I wish my teachers showed more concern for my learning. Also I would have liked to have an opportunity to take commerce as one of my school subjects. That we did not do that sort of subject the teachers should've advised me on going to further education as an alternative. My younger brothers must have had teachers with the same attitude as mine. Though they are a bit wayward the school could have done more for them. On the other hand Black kids at school should do more to help themselves, though after hearing my brothers talk I wonder how relevant the things they do at school are?

My experience of education has given me some insight into school and I think that I am now better able to help my daughter through school. Personally at some stage I will also like to pick up the threads of my education. Perhaps something like word processing to increase my job prospects or English and History because I enjoy both subjects.

Pauline felt that if her parents had had a better understanding of how to take advantage of the schooling available, she would have benefited; and that this would also have been true for her brothers, who followed her. This lack of understanding, a school geared to low standards, which saw Black children only in terms of their sporting potential, formed the background for Pauline's early education. To leave school early in order to earn a living seemed the only possibility at the time. The absence of a disciplined approach to school life, a comprehensive careers service, and information on post-school education are all areas of regret in Pauline's schooling. She feels she is now able to capitalise on this misfortune for her daughter's benefit. She also holds the view that Black children are not blameless in their failure at school. Pauline however, links this lack of success to the irrelevance of school work for them.

The regret she shows at not getting more out of education than she did is a motivating factor for her to return to education. She looks forward to doing this, either in the form of vocational or non-vocational learning.

The school's interest in sport and a lack of strictness in teaching were major factors in her secondary schooling.

Careers advice was available though all the alternatives were not known.

Some knowledge of further education could have been useful.

CASE HISTORY 19 : RUPERT GLOVER

Born and educated in England. The first of three brothers and the third child. Rupert's secondary education was at an E.S.N. school, the point at which he decided to begin his story. However, 'Special' is the name given to E.S.N. Rupert and his family interpreted special to mean obtaining additional educational advantage. The facts were not made clear to them.

WHEN I HEARD I was going to the special school, I was very sad because I knew I was going to leave my friends. I did take a test before I went there, and I suppose I must have failed. I felt very different when I was chosen for that school, I cried. I look back on it now and realise I used to write a bit slow, especially taking things off the board, I still couldn't understand it really, because there were others, for example, a couple of White kids who were slower than me; but they let them go on to higher school. My first day at this new school was really different, and difficult. I was confused. There were kids in this special school who were handicapped and I thought, what am I doing here? When I got settled into the school I found the teachers and pupils to be all right. We spent a lot of time going on outings, and I liked that. We also had a lot of classes where we did things like carpentry, and that. After a few years there, the woodwork teacher found me a job as an apprentice joiner. My time was split between college and on the job labour; a block release system.

At college I was the only student from that school and the only Black person in the class. As you will expect a lot of them had certain ideas about Black people, but that did not bother me. I am willing to talk to anybody, Black or White, but you got some stupid people in this world; most of the time they opened their mouth and obviously don't know what they are talking about. People like that are real ignorant, I just steer clear of them. One bloke in particular kept picking on me, but I soon sorted him out. I did very well in my practical woodwork and was praised for it, but I was told that my theory was not up to their standard, so I lost the opportunity to finish the apprenticeship. At the time it hurt, because I love woodwork, and I knew I could be a good carpenter. I could not see why the theory thing was so important. I was left without anything and ended up on the dole. I would prefer a job, but it is the same thing every time I go down to the job centre; nothing doing.

After a while I got into the Rasta religion. I have learnt a lot since as it has explained many things for me. Things haven't changed on the work front. People tell me I won't be given a chance because of my dread, but I tell them I did not get one before I went dread. People are not interested in my ability they only see my dread. They think because I have dread something's wrong with me. Living in England, you know, walking down the street with so many eyes looking at me, I know I am not free. I've met a few people who understand. One of my teachers at the special school was a good bloke. He spent a couple of years in Jamaica and when he came back he used to talk for hours. He got into the language and that sort of thing, and at least he is trying to understand. Within myself, I don't think I am that slow, to deserve what this society's done to me. I mean school is not everything. To live people have to have common sense and a lot of them don't have any.

The school never taught me my history, history about people like Marcus Garvey. I learnt my history since I became a Rasta and I am proud of my race and our achievements. The school only told me about White Kings and Queens, who don't mean much to me. I got to know myself kinda late and I am sad that I did not know earlier. I am interested in doing any sort of work if anybody will have me. Education is useful, but only if people get a break afterwards. I mean, I don't mind going back on a course or something but there aren't any for people like me.

His parents noticed, and he felt, he was a bit slow in
such areas as reading. They however said to him that
there was no cause for concern, though they were racked
with worry of the stigma on the family. It is important
to note that neither the school nor those concerned with
special schooling contacted the family until the
eleventh hour and this caused further anxiety.

That Rupert was confused and felt that he should not be
sent there indicates the stress and anxiety the family
experienced at that time. Rupert admits to being slower
than some of his classmates, but certainly not all of
them. The decision of the authorities was accepted as
the family did not know what could be done. (This
experience of hopelessness in response to educational
policy decisions is recorded in Bernard Coard's work
'How the West Indian child is made educationally
Subnormal in the British school system.') The handicap
label was a difficult burden for the family to bear.

Surprised at being chosen for 'special school' undermined his self confidence and negatively influenced the family's view of themselves.

Post-school education seen as more worthwhile than earlier schooling.

CASE HISTORY 20 : CHRISTOPHER GLOVER

Age seventeen, born and educated in England, Chris is the last boy and child in the family. He attended the same primary and secondary school as his brother and sister.

    I DID NOT always get on with some of the staff at the secondary school, mainly to do with behaviour. They used to make differences betwen the White lads and us; for example, I was told that I could not wear jeans, but they let the White lads wear them; making silly excuses for their decisions. Other members of the staff were great in their general approach, but I think they could have pushed me a bit more. We did C.S.E's instead of 'O' levels. I took Maths, English and Commerce, and got good grades in them. The careers man came the year before I finished school and advised me to go to a youth training scheme to start during the summer. He also told me that if I wished I could choose to go on to further education college.

The first scheme I went on was packing shirts into boxes. This was boring and I did not see any future in it, so I left. I then went to the centre and was given information for another scheme. I rang the firms and went in for a test and interview, and was accepted. This job was in an office dealing with paper work. I enjoyed that much more. While at this firm I applied to the further education college and was accepted on their D.E.C. general scheme. If I do well enough I will go on to do the D.E.C. National course, and hope to get some sort of job in management.

Looking back on my school life I feel that parts of it were worthwhile as it gave me the basic ideas for getting into a career in management. I still feel that the teachers should be more demanding; they must also show less favour to some kids and be more strict.

A careers service existed which was useful in some senses in that they provided information.

CASE HISTORY 21 : KEN NOBLE

The headmaster of Tulse Hill Comprehensive School near Brixton, London. He was born and educated to secondary level in Trinidad. Mr. Noble is one of only two Black headmasters in state secondary schools in England and Wales.

I **STUDIED FOR** my B.A. Degree (joint Hons. Spanish/Psychology at the University of Cork, Ireland. Ireland was chosen as the place to read for this degree by the Presentation Fathers who staffed the college I attended in Trinidad. Having completed my studies in Ireland I returned to Trinidad where I taught for seven years. During that teaching period I decided that I wanted to pursue post-graduate work and enrolled on a course at the University of Liverpool. Following my post-graduate year I did some teaching in Liverpool for about four years. I then obtained a teaching post at a London comprehensive school. Not the school I am presently at. By this stage I had completed a further post-graduate course in Education Technology and felt it necessary to take my teaching Diploma as I had no professional teaching qualification. Since that time I have started a Ph.D. project (about three years now) but that is on the shelf at present due to my workload. During that period I moved to about three different schools, being head of house in my last one. I later secured a headship, followed by this post at Tulse Hill.

The academic life at University in Cork was very sharp, and I soon realised that I had to work on my own and not be spoon fed as I had become accustomed. There were quite a few students from overseas, all from countries with a Catholic influence, and many of them Black. At Liverpool university I quickly realised that research is a lonely task. I was left alone, my only contact with the university was my tutor, who at first I seldom saw. He however completely directed research operations, and getting to know him later on I found that he was an excellent man. I will always remember him as he took an interest in me beyond actual tuition. He treated me as an individual and took much more than a casual interest in the work I was doing.

Arriving in London to teach I soon realised that even though England is one country, people in the different parts of the country are quite different. In Liverpool I found the children in school (my class) much more candid. They have a sharper sense of humour and in a way they moved closer to me in terms of a pupil-teacher relationship. This was manifest in the degree of sadness when I left. I was the only Black person in that school and my experience of race relations there was good. Racism was not manifest in their conduct towards me as I found the staff very supportive. There are some who I will always remember for the kindness they showed me.

This all changed when I came down to London. It was a different scene. The children were different in terms of their relationship, and attitude to staff. Their attitude was one of condescension. By this I mean, if I were a person with a chip on my shoulder I would have felt the same thing in Liverpool. I am referring here of my instantaneous impression within the first few weeks of having been in a London school. In this school some of the staff deliberately undermined my authority. I felt that such behaviour was unprofessional. On the whole I was not given the support that I got in Liverpool, as a result, I had to change my approach in dealing with disciplinary matters regarding the students. I was something of a mystery to some of the boys and some of the teachers, in the sense that there was always good discipline in my class: regardless of how the boys behaved in other classes. One of the things I personally held to and still hold is that I have never been late for a class. I will always be there when the students arrive. I found problems that existed outside my class took longer to sort out, though I would not jump to conclusions and say that the students' behaviour towards me was because of my race, as some White teachers had similar experiences. There were lots of things the hierarchy of the school closed their eyes to, hoping that it will go away. As a result I devised my own system of discipline, so the boys knew they had to work when they came to my class.

At my second school in London there was also a large percentage of Blacks, Asians, Cypriots and so on, but a larger proportion of Whites. The school was a challenge, not only educationally, but also with regards the degree of vandalism, which was appalling. In the end the boys were a little more circumspect in their behaviour. I think I got my second London post in part due to my record in teaching and maintaining discipline at my last school. There I ran a very good house. I will however, say yes to the question that my race featured in the interview. One of the questions that came up, and to some extent stumped me, was to what extent did I think that being Black will make a difference to my work in the school? In replying I said that I hoped my employment will not be because I am a Black man; because I see myself as a man who happens to be Black. The post requires someone with the right personality and one who will deal with school situations in a professional way. It is not just a question of colour. I got the post even though I was up against some really good candidates. Having secured my appointment I set about the following:

1. Creating the proper atmosphere in the school, e.g. cleaning up the place and so on.
2. Make both staff and students feel respected and wanted.
3. Convey to staff the feeling that they have my support.

I like to think that I did create a good impression in my
last post. This present post became vacant, and I applied
for it. Like a lot of heads I was welcomed with a certain
amount of caution, reserve and suspicion. Maybe because I
was not known to anyone in the school, though they may
have heard of me as I had taught in a school nearby.
Generally things have settled down nicely for all of us at
the school. One of the special features of this school is
the post-sixteen section.. Special, in that we operate a
consortium with two other schools. One is mixed and the
other a girls school. Together we offer about twenty
seven different courses at sixth form level. In addition
to that we have a number of link courses with further
education colleges in the area. My students could choose
from well over thirty subject areas. We are also in the
process of offering 'on site' additional courses aimed
mainly at the unemployed and low achieving sixteen year
olds. The courses will be in printing, computers,
painting and decorating and so on. Evidence from our
catchment area suggests a need for such courses.

A high percentage of our children come from the
Brixton area, and others come to us from as far as Crystal
Palace and Surrey. Some high achievers others not. On
the question of achievement and non-achievement of Black
children. This is something I feel very strongly about
for two reasons. Firstly achievement and under
achievement are not confined to Blacks. Nobody complains
about under achievement in the private sector of
education, and to a similar extent in church schools. Why
is it there are so many complaints about the state sector.
The answer is quite obvious, it is a question of low
expectations. At this school we have a good record of
getting boys to further and higher education, but that is
only one aspect. There are, however, very many capable
boys (bands one and two) who fail to achieve anything.
Sometimes leaving school without taking an exam, or in
some cases the results of their exams are of a very low
level. We are at present looking at a scheme of
monitoring every boy in the school, and if we ever get
that implemented and people are professional about
implementing it I think we will see a remarkable change in
the standard of education in this school.

At another level, I am much interested in Adult
Education (post-school) especially from my own experience.

I understand that in Sweden they encourage people to continue their education up to near the time of death. I feel that education ought not to be cut off at any point. We should always be looking to learn whether it be vocational or non-vocational. Education in the formal sense can help eradicate racism, though some of the most educated men are racists. It depends on one's understanding of the situation. Education with a small 'e', that is, getting to know about and understand people is also very important. This brings me on to the question of race relations. It is something that has to be looked at in context of the society we are in. Britain, even though it is said to be a multi-cultural society, faces many problems different from that of for example the United States. Britain has always been multi-cultural. The Romans, Normans, Saxons etc. Throughout that time a sprinkling of Blacks existed though not in significant numbers to make any great impression on the country.

The biggest factor in the history of this multi-cultural society is the slave trade. This country or significant parts of it was built on revenue received from the slave trade, though Blacks were not of major concern for people here as relationships were, for the most part, conducted in the colonies. Time has changed; things such as migration to this country changed the emphasis. British society having to relate face to face with the descendents of those slaves. Because of the attitude which the colonial power engendered some people are finding it very hard to come to terms with Black people as equals. They are still inclined to see the Black person negatively.

Multi-cultural education will go some way to assisting understanding of this area. I don't wholly agree with some of the definitions and approaches put forward, but a number of education authorities are taking this on board and it is a start. What has happened on the streets of this country has opened the eyes of the government to what they see as a problem. The pace has stepped up because the generation today are not willing to accept the sorts of attitude which our forefathers tolerated. They will not put up with it, not even from the law. I think the government realises that it is a battle they cannot win and as a consequence they are trying to do something. Where racial intolerance and racial conflagration exist it is news. The politics of such situations have very far reaching consequences, not only in education but in general relationships and trade. Again, multi-cultural education could go some way to improving understanding.

Adult education has a role to play in this though not the sole role as what is happening in society cannot be totally placed at the door of adult education. We are faced with a particular problem of a large amount of unemployed youths, especially Black youths. They need to be participating in something constructive. By the same token it will be wrong to create the impression in the minds of youngsters that because they are doing a particular course, through adult education they will get a job on completion of the course. Perhaps an input in their adult education programme should be education for leisure which can be gainfully used in their spare time.

The suggestion that adult education exists because the school has failed the Black person, and other groups is not quite correct. I would say that it will take youngsters of character to swim against the tide. In spite of everything I believe that if youngsters really wanted to make it in school they could. There are for example many young Blacks, about one hundred and twenty, leaving this school every year. I would say that about twenty will be seen as failures in the academic sense. Now, the failure of these youngsters starts in the third and fourth years and though the school has a contributary factor in their failure the wider community must also share the blame. The community fails to set and demand standards in concert with those the schools are trying to maintain. I realise that there will be a certain amount of resentment from the youngsters because few accept the discipline; but discipline and self-control are central to success. Because some boys are unwilling to accept this discipline and because some teachers are not willing to demand or to enforce it; is the reason why we have so many under achievers. Youth clubs and churches can play a part in conveying this attitude though to my mind the churches, except for a few, do not play as important a part as they could. The family, particularly immigrant families, are likely to have both parents working - as do some White families - or are single parents. Therefore, the family may find it difficult to help, though they will like to. This wish to help may also not be possible to achieve especially in the academic sense, as many parents are unfamiliar with some areas of work going on in schools today, e.g. computers. However, information does exist, willing parents to help, especially in the formation of the correct attitude in their children. It is therefore not correct for the public to say that information on education is not readily available.

As one of the few Black headmasters I do not see myself as a role model or missionary. I think, the fact that Black boys in the school know who I am, and they know that they can walk into my room at any time is good. This is the same for the White boys in the school. Because of the particular needs of this society I could see that my appointment to this school could have that side effect. Though, principally, I will like to think that I was appointed to this school as any other appointment to any headship to a particular job. In doing this job I realise that there are certain problems facing the school. The school as part of the community and race, are aspects of the schools' problems. It is a difficult task trying to bring people together. We can only hope for a great deal of understanding and persuasion that good sense will prevail.

I am a dedicated educationist and as such I am very concerned about the distress caused among some of the youngsters by society at large. By that I mean boys who are well qualified, and go for jobs and are still, in this day and age, turned away because of their colour. That is a factor I have to face and acknowledge. It is one of my major concerns. My other concerns are about relationships in the wider community, regarding feelings of belonging. Though some Black boys in the school and the wider community occasionally turn to crime, the police have been known to pick up many boys who are innocent; and that is regrettable. I say this because it is my personal experience. Barriers have to be broken down with regards the police. There are those who will resent this, but Black people are part of this society and the police will also remain as part of the society. If the two groups are going to be there, they might as well be brought together. We also hope that instead of giving lip service to race relations in this country, the government will do something very sincerely about it, as a lot of what is now happening is not really sincere.

The strict and self disciplined education received in the Caribbean and in Ireland laid the foundation for his success and his attitude to education.

In his situation, information on study and career prospects were readily available.

As a Black teacher in Liverpool he experienced no feedback. In London it was the exact opposite.

Strict professional monitoring of student performances is seen as one way of combating failure at school.

He does not see himself as a missionary nor as a role model.

CASE HISTORY 22 : TREVOR CARTER

Born in Trinidad, he arrived in England in 1954 to further his education. Presently employed as a senior co-ordinating officer with the I.L.E.A.; he was also a member of the Rampton-Swann committee on 'The education of West Indian children in British schools'.

THOUGH MY PARENTS were poor we lived in an area not far removed from many important people on the island, including the family of the late Prime Minister, Dr. Williams. Because of this I was in the catchment area of a primary school that produced notables like the Naipauls and Roy Newholm, the present General Secretary of the World Council of Churches.

In 1940 I went on to secondary school, this had to be paid for as I did not win a place at the premier college in the island, Queen's Royal. Places at Tranquility Boys, the other prestigious school for non-Catholics, were filled, so my parents sent me to a private school which was the brainchild of two radical educationalists, J. Edgar Moore and Hope Braithwaite, who had previously taught at Queen's Royal. The school was organised on British grammar school lines, but they created a system of linking themselves with the community, banned corporal punishment and created the house system. I was a bright and popular lad at school though I did not exploit the former. I also founded the school magazine, **Modern Times,** and was its editor for some time. I took the senior Cambridge G.C.E.''O' level exams and passed in five subjects. I therefore had to leave school for two reasons. One, that I did not do well enough to proceed further and two, I had to assist my parents financially as the eldest of the children.

My first job was as an office boy in a hardware firm. This shocked my parents due to the educational investment they had made in me. I recognised that I had to make a contribution and felt that there was no sin in work. This lasted for six months when I was fired due to my requests for higher wages. I then got a job as an assistant to a quantity surveyor for eighteen months and following that I joined the telephone company, getting heavily involved in its trade union activities. As a result of this I was transferred to another part of the island. Through contacts I had an offer to go to sea. This meant working on a commercial line which at that time was very lucrative. It also gave me an opportunity to see other parts of the world. I joined as a mess boy and moved up to able bodied seaman in three years. Our journeys were mainly to the United States and Guyana. The experience increased my sense of community, though it also brought me in touch with racism when we visited New Orleans. The experience taught me that the fight is against certain structures built by human beings and not human beings themselves. In order to make progress we have to dismantle structures that were built to perpetuate human suffering. I remain with that political conviction. For example, education in this country was created without Black people in mind and that leads me to the conclusion that the present structure must be made to reflect among other things, the presence of Black people in the U.K. Having spent three years at sea I found it difficult to accept work of a lower status than those who were schooled with me. My parents still held the idea that a job in the civil service or other such white collar work, was the type of occupation that I ought to get. Something socially acceptable.

To catch up on my education I went to the Royal Victoria Institute on evenings to study Architecture, a choice of profession influenced by my father as he was a builder. I also took a correspondence course through the International Correspondence School. It was also in my mind to go to England to study, as many people were now arriving back from England as qualified people and getting good posts. So, I left for England in 1954. On arrival I registered for evening classes having received information about such classes from a family friend, already established in England. I also got a labouring job to enable me to live, as no other jobs were available. It was difficult to get into any post with training facilities or any semi-skilled jobs. The trade unions were against it. The institutions of power debarred people like me from such opportunities and as such maintained racism.

I enrolled on a two year 'A' level course as a preliminary to studying Architecture and in what little free time I had, I got involved in trade union affairs. I took an active part in what was then called the Caribbean Labour Congress and the League of Coloured People. We kept in touch with developments in the West Indies especially British Guiana, as many of us felt that our duty was not to further our studies but to organise Black people to take part in the international working class struggle. We were naive and felt that capitalism and imperialism were structures that could easily be knocked down. In devoting myself to this cause I gave up studying, returning to it in 1958. I found it just as difficult when I started back. I had a full-time job, I maintained my interest in trade unions and I had a family to care for. I was later hospitalised for eight weeks due to a ruptured ulcer. I jettisoned the idea of architecture and pursued an interest in economics and politics through 'A' level studies. After one year I had to give this up as I spent a lot of time in Eastern Europe as a council member of the World Federation of Democratic Youth. I remained a registered student and this meant

that national service was deferred. I had no wish to join
the forces as the wars being fought were against Black
people in Kenya and peoples from Aden, Cyprus and
Malaysia. On returning to England I was invited to teach
in Guiana by the P.L.P. (Peoples Labour Party). The
school was organised to produce political cadres for the
party from local young people. The bright ones were sent
abroad to study. I stayed for three years and noted that
the loss of life was the end result of racism. I was
involved with the opposition party who lost the election
and I was asked to leave the country. While in Guiana I
leant how to deal with ideas and issues and was better
able to grasp essentials of a debate. It was a learning
situation for me. I was also advised to get 'a piece of
paper' (qualification) in anything, as it does not matter
how right my views. If I haven't that piece of paper
people will never take me seriously. That is the reality
of life, especially in the West Indies.

On return to England my wife supported my ideas to
study. She also applied to the post office for a job for
me as a telephone operator. This meant working at night
so I had all day to study. I enrolled at North London
Polytechnic to take 'O' levels, as I was refused an 'A'
level course because my passes in 'O' levels (Cambridge)
were not merit ones. I took four 'O' levels, got them and
went on to Kilburn Polytechnic to take three 'A' levels.
Law, Economics and Sociology were the ones I chose and I
got Economics and Sociology. My intention was to go on to
University to read Sociology but I realised that my grades
were not good enough to get me into the prestigious L.S.E.
I was unable to go to university outside London due to my
family commitments. The Polytechnic of North London
offered me a place on their teaching studies programme
which I took and gained a certificate. As a mature
person with my sort of experience I saw things quite
differently from other students and staff at the
Polytechnic. This made for some interesting debates
especially with the sociology staff who on the whole
related well to me and my ideas. I took an active part in
student union affairs and was instrumental in getting the
academic board to discuss a change in the syllabus to
represent Black studies. This issue was discussed but
never made part of the syllabus.

On one of my teaching practices I met Chris Searle,

who had recently returned from Trinidad.   Chris through
his work as a teacher published some of his pupils' poems
which showed the racism that existed in schools.   He was
sacked for this and the children came out on strike to
support him.   Because of the situation in the union had to
support him and he was reinstated.   His experience taught
me that in education I must start where the kids are
located as this is the only way.

My second teaching practice was in Hackney.   This
must have been successful as I was invited to take up a
full time post and was given responsibility for the
commerce section.   In my second year I was made deputy
housemaster.   The headmaster realised that there were no
Black teachers in a school that had more than fifty per
cent Black children, my appointment was to redress the
balance.   My relationship with the rest of the staff was
not really amicable but we agreed to disagree - a
love/hate relationship existed.   The parents of White kids
that I came in contact with received me well.   This was to
some extent due to my trade union background and my
knowledge of working class language and culture.   I stayed
in that school for ten years and learnt that to change
things, as I was not popular with my colleagues, meant
getting support from the community.   This move also meant
that the parents and children were not strangers to those
who provided a service and the buildings in which these
tasks were performed.   They were encouraged to see the
teachers and buildings as part of their community.   I also
joined the local C.R.C. in 1974, formed an education
committee and was its first chairman.   Luckily at that
time the local C.P.O. (community relations officer)
Elizabeth McGovern was very supportive.   A very articulate
person with extensive research experience, she was
invaluable to the cause.   As a group we introduced a
multicultural input in Hackney's syllabus.   We were
injecting change into the education system and at this
stage of the committee's life we were more influential in
the education division than the headmasters of the
schools.

All those things led to an invitation from the
California State Education Board for me to speak at a
conference on the education of Black people.   As a school
teacher I was able to speak directly to heads of division
in an attempt to influence changes in the curriculum.   My

activities on the committee led to my getting a fellowship for a year at the University of London's Institute of Education. In that year I was able to collect my thoughts and arrive at what I saw as the Black perspective in education. Being involved with Rampton-Swann and the C.R.C. I became well known and found that the staff and the head of the school where I worked became antagonistic. They perhaps found it difficult to come to terms with that they termed a 'black upstart'. If I had worked within their framework and their thinking and become part of the team that would have been all right, but their historical racism could not deal with the changing situation of Blacks, by Blacks. I found it difficult to work with colleagues with such attitudes. The atmosphere was not right to develop anything, especially education; and two things happen to a teacher in this position. Either he or she becomes weaker in their job through a sense of persecution, or he or she becomes a stronger and more determined person. It's like going to prison for political reasons. Either the prison regime breaks you or your personality becomes strengthened. Mine was the latter, and my strength was the community. The parents supported me, and even some White teachers, who recognised the need for change gave their support. That meant a lot to me. What I decided from this was that in order to be a good teacher I had to embrace three things. First, to get the consent of the kids; second, to have ideas on what education should be and third, to attempt change through community. There is no point going into school and standing in front of a class talking. The community and its needs must be part of my thinking. This point on community is very important. Because we are not living in a Black society, but a multi-ethnic one, the support of all groups are essential whether they be Cypriots, Welsh or Asian.

At this time I also became chairman of the National Association of Black Teachers and also formed a local C.T.A. (Caribbean Teachers Association). The icing on the cake was the organisation of a Black teachers conference in Hackney. At this conference we put forward certain proposals which made media headlines. It meant that when re-organisation and amalgamation came the powers that be recognised the Black presence in its deliberations.

My fellowship year was spent putting all those sorts

of things together. The fellowship was organised by the
I.L.E.A. (Inner London Education Authority) through its
multi-ethnic inspectorate.   It is awarded to persons
participating in changes in education to provide some
thoughts and ideas that would lead to policy statements
for multi-cultural education.   There are five fellows
every year. The job that I am presently doing, in a way I
helped to create.   As part of I.L.E.A's multi cultural
policy on education (1977), consultation with minority
communities was recommended, so we worked on a structure
of how to deal with this consultation. One of the ideas
was that there should be education liaison officers, paid
by I.L.E.A. to work within and facilitate the community;
and to use the community to help change the education
facility. I.L.E.A. appointed three such officers, as part
of a pilot scheme. One in Westminster, one in Tower
Hamlets and one in Lambeth. This was so successful that
the authority saw the need for one in each division, but
states that there should be a senior person to co-ordinate
all these posts.   Winston Best was the first person to
hold that post. He later became an inspector of primary
schools and I succeeded him. My team consists of twelve
workers, not all Black.

My aim in the job is to assist in dismantling racism
in education and those institutions which support racism.
The attempt is to change attitudes with the participation
of the community.

1) To try to get Black teachers to relate to their
community.

2) To change in their 'heads' to the view that they
are not only teachers. Though we are few we have to give
back to our community that which came from them. Our
skills etc. As teachers we are the most articulate and
must voice the fears and hopes of Black people. They have
invested leadership in us.

The usefulness of education depends on how it is
seen. As far as I am concerned I found education useful
in the following three ways; first, it liberated me
intellectually. Second, it gave me the tools to help my
own community and third, it is still the most important
vehicle for change in terms of status and occupation.

Because of my political background I see education in
terms of a transference of the dominant culture to those
being educated.   This dominant culture as far as Black

people are concerned is racist and the dominant culture will not devise an education system to change society fundamentally, and therefore we who are at the bottom rung find that in order to participate more fully we will have to change things. Education is central to this change. This means Black people have to master the dominant culture and effectively modify it so that it addresses itself to our needs. This is nothing new, the working class and Marxists in this country always tried to do that and comprehensivation, despite all its drawbacks came from that dual source. The tripartite system was not in the interest of working class children and it had to go.

My view is that the presence of a number of Black pupils in this society will fundamentally reform this society. We are already witnessing this as the presence of Blacks as students and teachers will make for reformation which we shall see in thirty years time, but what is happening now is that while working class culture never had entree to schools, Black people have. Multi-culturalism forms the vanguard for this. Multi-cultural education is a teacher concept, if you were to ask any Black parent about that they would say, I don't know what you are talking about. What I want to know is that my children are getting a good education. The concept of multi-cultural education means good education. That is, a concept devoid of racism and on education that recognises that what the kids bring into school is valuable. Teachers have to recognise and respect such values and orientate themselves and their thinking to this fact. The policy makers recognise the value of multi culturalism, which some see as a threat. It means that policy makers may not always be sympathetic to changes brought on through multi-culturalism. Teachers will, therefore, have to unpack what the policy makers give them and use it to truly teach multi-cultural work. Multi-cultural education came from the early days of Black studies programmes (1974-1977) and the Black Power struggles in this country and the United States. It meant something which influenced the whole curriculum. All ideas and policy statements originate and are founded on such early thoughts; though they may not reflect it.

The situation in London is different from other parts of the country as far as Blacks and education are concerned. As the capital it tends to be the leader in policies on education and race, because of its location and its resources.   All L.E.A.'s have their education department, but I.L.E.A. is one massive education authority.   Also the existence of a large population of Black people and their historical influence sets London apart, even from cities like Liverpool and Cardiff.   In Liverpool and Cardiff Blacks have made little impact in city life.   In London they make their presence felt. Further, the I.L.E.A. spends a lot on Adult Education.   At present they are encouraging people to participate and those who participate in that sort of education are the very people who will participate in trade unions and so on, the old and the middle aged who took part in that sort of education are into politics.   People like Russell Profitt and Paul Boateng.   Education attempts to create a passive society, and this system has been fairly successful with its working class.   Black people arriving in this country were quite prepared to enter and participate as equals because they came out of that education system which taught us to be docile.   Unemployment, and hurdles against integration we had to face.   It followed that Black people had to create their own methods of dealing with such hostile environment.   The system cannot deal with our children.   The fact that Black parents, brothers and sisters came home from work and complained of the treatment they got at work, meant that the young ones while not being told, listened to the parents/family's anger.   This gave the kids a new value system which says oppose, confront and fight.

Our Black generation is unique because this system offered us nothing in order to make us feel part of this society.   By alienating us the only things of value our kids have to relate to are issues like the Cuban revolution, Angola, Zimbabwe, Rastafarianism and so on. There is nothing inside of this culture to attract us, nothing.   We have no heroes, the Benns, the Thatchers mean nothing.   There are few intellectuals who talk on our behalf, people like Stuart Hall, and they are isolated in pockets of academia.   We have not been able to show ourselves and there is a high distrust by our own Black people and quite rightly so, against those of us who succeed.   We have not developed a Black psyche as have our Black American brothers and sisters.   We have not because our churches have not yet consolidated to educate the community.   In the U.S.A. Jesse Jackson through the church created havoc with the sales of Coca Cola when the company sacked some Black workers. He used the pulpit to inform people of this and instructed them to refuse to buy Coca Cola. They did as he asked until the workers were re-instated.

The Black community must get rid of the notion that the schools are there for our interest, but controlled by teachers. The community has to own the schools. When this is done we will no longer have to provide supplementary schools. For the time being our Black supplementary schools must come to grips with the fact that they have to supplement what is going on in schools. The schools must not only give traditional lessons but must inform the kids why this is happening, tell them what is going on in the country and how to deal with and change the situation.

Similarly, the idea or reality of a Black full-time school. Though it is seen by some as an emotional response to the failure of White institutions, it may be a move in the right direction given the present circumstances. There is no idealogy in blackness so one must mean a school of Black teachers and Black kids. But who can say that the Black school teacher will do the things he or she ought to do? They could be reactionary. The experience of the U.S.A. show that in those schools you tend to have a number of people who are highly alientated, criminalised etc.

Creating Black schools is dividing the school from the community. Education is only good if it is a communal thing.

His move from teaching to administration with the I.L.E.A. was the result of his involvement with multi-cultural programmes and other educational initiatives.

He sees I.L.E.A's lead in anti-racist programmes and adult learning schemes as beneficial to the whole country.

For him the Black person's belief that education is the key to improved status and quality of life is a true one.

CASE HISTORY 23 : KELVIN CARBALLO

A specialist teacher from Trinidad employed by the I.L.E.A. as a curriculum development officer. A post that emerged as a result of the Rampton-Swann committee's finding on West Indian children. The development and organisation of supplementary schools are his main interest outside his occupational commitment.

MY EARLY EDUCATION meant little to me as I had no concept of what it was or what it was supposed to do. I never had a desire at that stage to learn anything at school. Later I was transferred to the Protestant school where my aunt was a teacher but did not enjoy it there. There was no system of checking on the schools kids attendance as you have today, so I left and joined my friends at their school. I was not the best behaved lad, and at that school I got strapped for being late. I did

not like it and took my books and left. I then went to San
Fernando Roman Catholic Boys' which was a bit better, but I
got molested by the bigger boys as I was not a Catholic. I
then skipped school for about two years and invented
homework to keep my family happy, and even asked my brother
to help me with it. On returning to the school I found the
rate at which I was following the text was faster than they
had done at school. I was doing fractions and percentages
before they were. Personally I wanted to leave school in
my early teens to be a motor mechanic. My mother could not
come to terms with that due to all the money she had
invested on me. My elder brother was at Presentation
College, the premier college in the south of the island and
as he was an excellent scholar my mother was able to get me
in without my taking the normal entrance exam.

At this time my approach to education and learning
meant that I stored things in my head. It had nothing to
do with the use of one's intelligence to unravel things. It
was all about memory. All through my educational
experience this is what learning meant to me. The end of
my first and second term I did very badly. In the second
year my grandmother as much as told me that I could never
be as bright as my elder brother, so I gave up studying
until 1962 when I came to England. On reflection I did not
do well in school in the West Indies as I felt rejected by
both my family and my school.

I came to England because my friends were leaving and
in the back of my mind I wanted to be involved in
education. Not so much to gain certificates, but for my
self-development. In 1965 I enrolled on a course
preliminary to taking O.N.C. The only information on what
was available and how to get it, was from my brother. I
went to the college personally to apply and was turned away
by the doorman who told me the preliminary course was full.
I had no idea that I ought to have gone to the course
information desk. I then got a job at the U.S. base
outside London so I had to give up the idea of study.
About a year later I was introduced to an African guy
called Aqua. He had a book on logic and invited me to look
at it. It seemed interesting and he advised me to take an
'O' level in it. I enrolled at North Western Poly (evening
class) and passed my logic. This gave me confidence and
made me feel that I was not a stupid man. In 1964 I left
the job at the base and enrolled on a full-time two year

'A' level course. I had saved up for this and went to the University Tutorial College in Tottenham Court Road. 'O' levels were £11 per subject per term and 'A' levels £17. Having obtained my 'A' levels I thought I could go on to do a degree not realising that subjects taken at 'O' levels do not count if also taken at 'A' levels. As a result I was rejected as no advice was available to me at that time. My alternative was to register at the North Western Poly to take a teacher's training degree. To say I learnt anything is doubtful, because the whole idea of how to approach work (studying) was still alien to me. There was no one at the college to give us any advice on approaches to study, how to read effectively, and so on. They assumed everybody knew how to go about studying. Though to my mind a good education requires that such skills be imparted. Biology was my main subject and I got a credit for it, though my overall classification was a second class Hons.

My first teaching post was at Ashmount primary. That is having refused to teach in a school that was of predominantly Black kids as I was very much against ghettoisation, feeling that I could teach in any school. At Ashmount I was given a class of kids termed 'disruptive', and coped reasonably well. In my whole teaching career, it is the only school where I had such wonderful co-operation. There was no racism in the obvious sense either from staff or students; and the parents I came in contact with related well to me. I felt they realised that the sorts of things I did with their children was what they wanted them to learn. I later left Ashmount to go to Grafton primary as I understood progress in the profession was to a large extent based on a wide teaching experience. The headmaster at this school was very much against any teaching that was not pure European. He never established a rapport with the Black kids in the school and singled out a female Indian teacher to express his dislike of the changing ethnic scene in education. I was successful in an application I made to teach in Nigeria and left the school after one term.

Nigeria at that time was in the throes of introducing free primary education for all and we had to cope with very poor facilities. I only stayed in Nigeria for nine months as I found it difficult to adapt to a country where nothing was familiar. Other than to take part in this new educational venture, I also went to Nigeria to tease out my roots.   While there I had time to re-think my life and where I wanted to go.   While in Nigeria I was forced into a situation where I was made to realise my ability.   I was made head of science in a school and had to organise teaching practice, remedial education and so on.   However, because I did not have a P.G.C.E. my salary was lower than those who had less responsibility and a P.G.C.E.   I decided to return to England.

On returning to England I went to teach at Robert Blair while I took my P.G.C.E. part-time and also did a short course retraining in maths teaching.   The results of my efforts were most rewarding and I was encouraged to read for my Masters degree.   The intake at Robert Blair was mainly the sons and daughters of the workers at Pentonville prison;   and there was the general view that many of those workers sympathised with the National Front.   The hostility the kids showed to me could therefore be put in focus, though they were hostile to any teachers putting forward any challenging ideas.   Even the headmaster had hostile responses from parents when he attempted to bring about change.   Racism in the profession certainly exists.   For example, I was praised for my work while at Ashmount.   As a scale I had produced the best dissertation in Biology at the Poly.   After a year at Ashmount a White lady teacher joined the staff and was soon given a scale III post in Science and I was not even informed nor invited to compete for the post.

I left Robert Blair and went to Pools Park Junior, a well kept school where I taught English as a second language.   I was made redundant from this school because of cuts (last in, first out).   Strangely, another member of staff who came in part-time to cover staff absences was not made redundant and took over my class.   As a result of all this I went back into my shell, because I put a lot into my posts and got nothing in return.   I then went to Hungerford Junior where an Indian headmaster presided.   Within a week of taking this class I fell in love with them.   Their reading was excellent, but their maths was poor.   I thought I'd do a blitz on maths, but two White parents complained to the head that I was giving too much maths.   The head called me into his office and told me of the complaint.   I defended the line I took, but the head did not support me. I thought the business of primary education was to develop the three 'R's but I was wrong.   The head undermined my professional judgement by withdrawing the two children from my class and taught them in his office. I felt betrayed, frustrated and angry.

Naturally I was happy to get my present job as it allowed me to leave that school. I am a member of a team which is essentially concerned with promoting 'good' teaching practice throughout I.L.E.A. schools. My specific role is to look at the home and school links and to try to find ways to encourage parents to participate in school life, without coming up against barriers. We visit schools and monitor their practices. We see ourselves as supportive to the school, providing them with the sorts of curriculum considerations that would give a better or wider view of education. Heads and teachers may see me and other members of the team as 'experts' and be covertly hostile. We are not there to tell them what to do.

So far we have been well received, primarily because the schools we work with were hand picked by the inspector and he is well aware of the nature of the project dealing with anti-racist policies. The teachers are willing to participate and many of them tell us of their problems of resources. Our success will not only be important to I.L.E.A. but for all of Britain. It is the first time a group of people are engaged in de-Eurocentraling education with the local authority's blessing. We do not want to see multicultural education as an appendage to what already exists. It must be part of all subject teaching. For example, from an historical point of view the contribution the Hindus made by injecting the zero (0) into maths or the Arabic notation of numbers, the quadratic equation by the peoples of the upper Nile etc.

Being a Colonial I would not say that I had received education in the West Indies as such, because I believe education to be the development of the critical mind such that you can relate to your environment and nature and note the contradictions in society. I was therefore not educated but schooled to fulfill a colonial role. As colonial peoples we have always seen education as an instrument by which we move out of the ghetto, out of poverty, and I thought that when a person qualifies he or she should be able to have 'steak on the table' more regularly. But the politics of this society is not such that could even make me feel that the qualifications I have are useful to me because of the institutional racism which exists. How many Blacks will obtain positions to (a) their qualification and (b) their ability? For this to happen we need more perceptive people in positions of power e.g. heads of educational institutions, Town Halls, Industry, Parliament and so on. For our part we have to have luck (be in the right place at the right time) political experience (how to play the organisational game) and a willingness to commit ourselves to the community as we can no longer stay isolated from what is happening there.

Also in thinking of changes. The school must cease to be places of 'holy ground' where only teachers can go to mystify children. It must be more open to the community and answerable to it. Because of the history of schools in England Black people, Jews and Chinese have to run supplementary schools to fully educate their children. Now supplementary schools must exist in so far as the schooling system in this country does not educate Black children adequately. The education the Black kids get is basically Eurocentric; we need to inject a balance. Until the education system can be modified and be honest enough to teach all children adequately there will be a need for supplementary schools. The supplementary school should concern itself with the development of political and social awareness, such that children can grow up knowing the society in which they live and knowing how to confront racism.

The disadvantage of such schools is that children should be developing their own interests. Going swimming, playing football, taking a trip to the countryside and so on. We should not have kids going to school six days a week as they may grow to resent education. The reason why I am part of a Saturday school scheme is to make it possible at some stage to get the schools to teach Black kids adequately. To prevent the kids from asking themselves 'Is there something wrong with me?'

The Curriculum Development project has the backing of the I.L.E.A. through their anti-racist document. This document neutralises the negative actions of heads and teachers who are against change. The hardened racist in schools, the person who squanders reason and who will not change his view in the light of new evidence; such a person will have to succumb and abide by the law of authority. An example of such a law working is the one which makes it an offence not to serve a Black person in a

pub. Some publicans may not like it but they have to abide
if they want to stay inside the law. Laws against racism
in education are not far away. Teachers will be answerable
on grounds of professional misconduct, like doctors to the
B.M.A.

The person to educate first is the unintentional
racist, i.e. a person who himself or herself has been
miseducated. Educated to believe that British and White is
best. Such a person uses the same rationale to dismiss
evidence opposed to their racist beliefs even when this
evidence is irrefutable.

This period of education we are witnessing in Britain
is a renaissance, a quiet revolution. I have great hopes,
and this is very important. Another major and complex
issue in this time of change is the argument for and
against Black schools. At this period in time we do not
want to lose another generation as we have already lost too
many. If Black schools can deliver the goods, such that
the kids can gain an expression to their lives and get
worthwhile employment, then by all means have Black
schools. There are Jewish schools and this did not make
them apart from the whole society. They saw the need for
it, and it serves them well. The problem with a Black
school will be one of economic power and academic validity.
It may also set up an elitist system within the Black
community and this will not be welcomed by the grass roots.
I am in favour of Black schools at this moment in time but
hope that there will be no need for it.

Black schools are a cry for a cultural voice and the
riots in Brixton and other cities were a manifestation of
that cry. Freire talks about 'cultural silence' in
colonial development. We have to some extent lived through
that and come out of it. The Black kids in Brixton and
elsewhere are doing just that. They are saying treat me
'fairly'. I personally prefer the word 'fairly' to
'equally' as we can all understand that. The concept of
equality is subject to too many interpretations and
misunderstandings. The Black person is saying, 'why should
I go through all these things and in the end I am not
respected as a person, I am not given the opportunity to
share in the wealth of the nation. I am not given the
opportunity to make a contribution to the society in which
I live, therefore forget education'.

I however believe that for all its faults education received can mean a higher standard of living and a fuller life.

His early education had no meaning for him. He felt his schooling lacked direction and interest.

His enrolment at evening class was followed by full-time 'A' level study. A lack of guidance at this stage was a crucial factor.

CASE HISTORY 24 : ORVILLE WOODFORD

Born and educated in the West Indies up to secondary level. He is an elder of the Seventh Day Adventist religion, and headmaster of one of their church schools. This school gained national prominence at its inception. Located in urban Tottenham, London, it is conveniently placed for the Seventh Day Adventist community who are for the most part Black. The school is staffed in the main by Black people with the majority of students of the same racial origin. As such the school is seen as the only all-Black school in Britain.

I **CAME TO** England in 1961 with the sole intention of going to university. I however found on my arrival that it was not easy to work and study as for example, in America. It was difficult to earn enough even during the holidays to enable me to study full-time. The work I got was mainly unskilled labouring, and this exhausted me and made it difficult to study after work. I decided to take the Civil Service exams, passed and joined H.M. Customs as a clerical officer. I later gained promotion, and commendation, but decided while there to switch from the Social Sciences to the Natural Sciences and then on, I hoped, to university. I then went to evening class taking 'A' levels in Physics and Chemistry. I still found working and studying hard, and this problem was magnified by the fact that, even though I was highly motivated, the classes I attended kept folding up due to a fall in numbers by January. I got fed up and decided to go full-time. I saved up for that purpose and in 1970 I resigned my job and went on to full-time education. I continued with Physics and Chemistry and added Maths. I later read for a degree in Physics, followed that up with a P.G.C.E. and later a Masters in Physics. I accepted my first teaching post in Hornsey at Secondary level and enjoyed that experience. It was noticeable that racism while not overt, was present. You see, British racism can be such a subtle thing that it is difficult to put our finger on it, and say, that is a racist act.

I came through situations where I strongly felt that the expectations of teachers influenced the results of their students. I was a recipient of that as a student and now I saw it happening to other pupils. Our results are not a reflection of our ability. Ability has something to do with whether the students are making it or not and my impression was that where the teachers felt the pupils were of a particular category, ability-wise, this came out as their grades. As a student there were no means available to me for dealing with this situation. There wasn't any political voice that was raised anywhere within education that I could relate to and ask for help. I and many others just had to take what was coming if we wanted to get through. The students union within the college and university did not concern themselves with these issues and there were no staff to turn to. As I said, the expectation problem is one which Blacks are affected by more than others. Some Blacks actually accept this view of themselves and function at that level. Black people must be schooled out of this and realise that they are quite capable of doing well. I did not see myself going for help to any person who really had a different perspective that would help me. That frustrated me. It also caused a large percentage of drop-outs, both Blacks and Whites from the system. I just managed to make it without that kind of support. That was not all as the usual problem of housing and so on existed, but that was the society at that time, and Black people knew what they were up against.

Careers advice was supposedly out there somewhere, but because I knew what I wanted I did not investigate. Careers information was not related to my course in any way. My introductory information on the education system in this country was obtained from libraries, so I suspected careers information was also in the library. I would say that education in this country and its meaning for me could be seen in two ways. The 'A' levels were a means to an end because I intended to teach, and the information I picked up at degree level did not bring about much change in me as I was already a person operating successfully in my church. I was an already formed person in a way and therefore no change was envisaged other than purely academic. University education was something I enjoyed rather than it doing something for me. The switch from Arts to Science was a good move. Perhaps it all made me more English?

It is difficult to see education as the single factor influencing racism in this country. There are a lot of factors producing the kind of society we live in, education is only one of them. Attitudes of those in authority, housing, social welfare are all part of it. To see education as a definitive answer is too simplistic. However the part it can play is certainly important. In this school we address ourselves to Adventism and the education of Black children. We hope to make a significant impact and in so doing contribute to the whole community.

Society gets its motivation from different things that interface into it. The politics of the day, what's happening in schools and other major institutions like the church. We the Seventh Day Adventists number about fourteen thousand in this country, and hence the ripples that it makes reaches the consciousness of the society. The Black settlers in this country, from the thirties and forties knew about Adventists from the countries from which they came. Secondly, we had Adventists schools in those countries and the lack of an Adventist school for their children in this country was something that concerned parents. It became somet hing that they could put up with while problems did not force them to rethink, but when children in schools began to adopt the new life style of this society one very different from their parents' expectation, the childrens' behaviour was seen as a problem. The drift away from the church was significant and this worried the parents. Their answer to why this was happening was that it was due to the schools. The schools changed their attitudes to family life, home, religion and so on. The family life of grandmother nearby, children leaving home after marriage had gone. This breakdown was significant to an Adventist family in a way that proves to be even more emphatic than an ordinary family. Their whole life style was changed.

Added to that was the fact that the newspapers began to publish the view that Black children were underachieving and leaving school at an alarming rate, virtually illiterate. The parents now had two causes for concern. Rejection of their life style and being ill-equipped to achieve anything in this society. That kind of pressure on the parents led them to believe that education was the culprit. Given this view of the situation the parents felt that the kind of facilities they had in the West Indies, like Adventists schools and an environment where they could practice their religion with honour was necessary. To be able to practice religion with honour was important. For example, if the child said he or she was going to church on Saturday this would not be strange. They would not be made fun of as seventy five per cent of their friends will be doing the same thing. In this way the child held values their parents and peers subscribed to. The parents also saw the need for the kinds of discipline, spiritual and temporal exercised in church schools. As a result parents put pressure on the church elders to find schools of the church. This began in 1960 and by 1971 discussions were ongoing. A view put forward at the time was that if the church had a school it will be totally Black. The reason for this is that when Adventists came to this country from the West Indies they settled in urban areas, especially London. Near to where universities, colleges and work existed; as they came either to study or work, often both. At present, ninety eight per cent of Adventists in urban London are Black. If I took you to any Adventist church in London you will think that it is a Black religion. Whereas any Adventist church outside London will be seen as a White

religion. Because of this, a school in the city will be a
Black school. The elders thought this would be a problem.
Would it be something that this society will find
acceptable? We also wondered if the authorities would even
allow it. As time went on the need outweighed all those
arguments. By 1977-1978 we were looking for sites to start
a school, while mounting a programme of supplementary
education which the I.L.E.A. partly financed.   That
basically is the background to the school.

    This project was really to meet a church need, but it
came at a point in time when society at large was becoming
very political about what was happening with Black
children.

    When we opened in 1980 the Rampton Report was coming
out and information from it made many Black parents see
this school as the answer to their problems.   I even
received a letter from the Conservative Party commending us
on the positive nature of our programme for Black people.
We received letters from all quarters and the media
focussed on us for a time. For the first time it was felt
that Blacks were doing something about a problem they
'appear' to have as a comunity. We knew we were addressing
a problem within the church, yet at the time the public saw
it in a wider context. The result of this was that the
parents of Black children in the area, Adventists or not,
wanted to send their children here.   Many parents stated
that where there is a school where many of the teachers
share the same cultural background as the children, they
would send their children to that school. At the present
time we have a waiting list of children wanting to get in.
Twenty seven per cent of our children are non-Adventists.
We agonised on this because we are aware of the threat of a
dilution of Adventism, but we have a duty to the community
and we do not want to exclude them.   In this school we
educate to sixteen and hope soon to introduce a sixth form.
At present our careers advice system begins when the child
is thirteen and continues to sixteen.   At each stage we
inject information consistent to their individual
development. For example, each child by fifteen will be
known by our careers teacher and the careers people at the
Borough. Our member of staff is solely responsible for
careers and works in tandem with the Borough staff.   We
have been sensitive enough not to hand over careers totally
to the Borough as we feel we know the child better. There

is a constant monitor of the child's ideas and their parents views. Also information is readily available on all aspects of our work at the school. We find that many pupils narrow their scope due to lack of information, this we continually correct. To achieve this we relate to a pool of local business people whom we hope will take students recommended by us.

There has also been a request from many Black people, especially parents. They ask us to put on evening classes and this is an area we are looking into. However, this aspect of Adult Education must come after we have developed the sixth form. It is interesting to note that this request exists even though the wider education service has evening classes. There is the willingness to come here and engage themselves in something constructive. This community link with the school with its religious influence is fundamental to some, and seen as a power base by others. The power base of the church school in the Black community exists, but is one that we have not exploited at all. The church tend to give politics a low profile, and it will be unusual in our church to push a political line. That is not to say that the church will be outside its province in doing that. If for example the church felt strongly that the Labour Party chose to close church schools, it will be totally within our right to erase this threat through mobilising our people against it. This will not be contradictory to the ethics of our religion.

Given the fact that we have a school that works, access to the media because of the special nature of the school, it is possible to make political statements. This will throw me in the political arena to operate for the benefit of Black people from a privileged base. I resist this because to get this place to function within the church needs total commitment. I am not blind to the Black dimension as the church and school activity demonstrates. Rightly we are addressing ourselves to the community needs and in that sense to the Black dimension.

Religion was, and still is, the central feature of his life. Education occupies a secondary position.

Full-time education to 'A' level was later followed by undergraduate and post-graduate study. He found higher education interesting; it helped him to better understand the British way of life.

The all Black school rapidly attracted the support of Black parents many of whom were not Adventists. There is now a waiting list.

He was early convinced of the significance of teachers' expectations of children as affecting their performance.

CASE HISTORY 25 : CLYDE CARTER

Born and educated in Trinidad, Mr Carter is the younger brother of Mr. Trevor Carter (Case History 22). Having successfully negotiated the education system in England and experienced teaching both in England and Nigeria he decided to return to his native country to teach.

I ENJOYED MY early years at school, up to about fourteen years of age. School then became a sort of factory system that prepared me for a job in the civil service. I did not complete this part of my schooling and did not get into the civil service. This was a disappointment to my parents. I left school because I was technically minded and the school was geared for the academically inclined student. Because I was not very good at academic subjects like English and French and so on, the teachers were not too keen on me. Because of that I was dissatisfied and left. At that time I was quite good at solving technical problems and fixing things, but there was no recognition for those sorts of skills. I suppose I would have liked to get into the civil service but I knew I did not have the qualities for that type of occupation.

At school I think the teachers saw it as their duty to our parents to get us qualified for the service. They must have figured that this was the sole reason why our parents sent us there. Unfortunately work in the technical field did not carry high status. At sixteen I saw an advert by our Railways Board for apprentices. It meant taking an open exam based primarily on secondary school work. I took the exam and came among the first twenty out of four hundred students. The railways was possibly one of the best technical training institutions I have ever come across. As a complete industry, I learnt many different skills such as fitting, turning, welding and so on. My immediate boss must have recognised the sort of struggle that existed in me, that is some apprentices accepted being a craftsman. I did not accept that and thought my boss felt the same. Though perhaps he was too old to change he did encourage me along the right lines. The apprenticeship scheme was modelled on the English system. This called for an understanding of a work culture that was English and was to prove useful to me later on. On completion of my apprenticeship as a diesel fitter, there was talk amongst staff and public that the railways system was under threat of closure. I also felt that opportunities for promotion were not on and being married I was worried about the future. I felt that the only way forward was to increase my education. Since this was not possible in Trinidad the next stop was England. England because that is where most people went to further their education.

In England I had the problem of knowing what course to follow, where to find it, and how to go about getting on it. I wanted to do a City and Guilds course as that type of work was part of my apprenticeship. However, most of the people I came across from the West Indies were doing non-technical courses and could not advise me properly. One of my brother's friends suggested that I go to the Regent Street Polytechnic and do O.N.C. in Engineering. I went along and the interviewer asked about my levels of qualification, and I told him of my apprenticeship. He then asked for any other educational experience. I told him of the Bennett College correspondence course I started and he felt that the commitment needed to embark on one of those courses plus my technical background made me suitable for a place. I then started my O.N.C. in Mechanical Engineering and later went on to H.N.C.

I struggled through the course, especially the maths component. Also, having to work during the day as a capstan operator added stress to my study situation. I persevered for six years part-time to complete my H.N.C. Fortunately my employers were sympathetic and allowed me time off to take exams and so on. At the Poly, at least on my course, there was only one other Black student, a Nigerian chap. He also worked very hard and was successful. Because of the rush to get to class from work and the rush to get home from class no one in the class related on a social level. What I had time for and did learn was that I had to come to terms with the system of education in this country. I found a problem with the college language, that is, understanding their thinking on concepts, and expression of it. I got over most of this by reading extensively; though it took me some time to get used to the lecturers' use of it. The lecturers were aware of my problem and were probably willing to talk to me if I went to them, but they did not offer any assistance. This was made more difficult as classes were from 6 p.m. and at 9 p.m. everybody wanted to go home. An advantage of the course was that all the lecturers were industry based and that experience made them easy to get along with. The language thing was however a setback which influenced my writing up of class and homework.

My other criticism of the Poly system at that time was the lack of advice and guidance to students on matters relating to careers and information for acceptance by the ruling professional body on completion of the course. For example, to belong to the Institute of Mechanical Engineering I had to do endorsements but was unaware of the regulations necessary to satisfy the institute's requirements. Staff at the Poly seemed to take it for granted that I and other students knew what was required. Also, none of my relatives or friends knew of anything in this field of study as I was the first in the group to attempt this sort of thing. Despite all the hassles and frustration I successfully completed the course. I was then forced to make a decision on my future without any professional guidance. Unfortunately, or maybe fortunately, as it turned out, the firm I worked for was shedding workers as things weren't too good for them. Teaching was one of the things I thought I would like to change to. Teaching my subject area. Secretly I guess I've always fancied teaching; this was perhaps due to my teachers in primary and later when I was an apprentice. They made an impact on me and I also saw them as figures of status and power.

My next step was to go to Bolton College of Education (Tech) for teacher training. Going to Bolton from London showed that I was not aware that there were other technical teachers training colleges about. For example, Garnett College in London. Had I known this it would have been better for me and my family. Again the lack of knowledge and advice was a disadvantage. Not that I did not enjoy Bolton but my family was in London and that meant emotional and financial strain.

Bolton was my first stab at full-time Adult Education. It was like a breath of fresh air, a release. This was my first pleasant experience of education since primary school. I was free from the pressures of a full time job and part-time education and the support I got from staff at the college was constructive and encouraging. I was the only West Indian student in that year though there were a number of other Black students about. The students in the college both Blacks and Whites got on very, very well. There were all sorts of activities organised by students and sometimes staff. Life at the college was quite good. I also received my first introduction of the tutorial system and that gave me an insight into what education could really do for a student. I found I was making a lot of comparisons between different forms of education, especially full-time and part-time, and what effect each had on student development. The full time course gave me an opportunity to understand the society I lived in, through conversation and community. Part time education to me was a continuation of what went on in Trinidad, that is being there and getting specific qualifications for a job. At Bolton staff tried their best to find out if I had problems, in fact they seemed to expect me to have problems, especially academic ones. I felt that it was because I came from a technical situation where problems of expression are expected to exist, or maybe because I was Black they might have felt that I did not get the rounded education my skilled White colleagues received. To me this latter point was more evident. They were not racist, never in an obvious sense. Indeed they went out of their way, most of them, to behave in non-racist ways. But their expectations of my performance was obvious. Let's say I did better than I thought they expected me to. This sort of reaction to the Black person seems to exist in all the levels of education I have participated in, in England. But then, we are dealing with people who knew how to be subtle if they want to.

At Bolton I was surprised to find careers as part of the course. They gave me a lot of assistance of how to go about getting jobs. This was organised so we could benefit from the experience of our fellow students who recently had interviews. Personal encouragement and lessons on interview skills were also given.

The move from a skilled shop floor worker to a lecturer in further education was a big one. Economically, in terms of status and especially psychologically it took some adjustment. I was the first Black lecturer to be appointed at this large north London technical college. I saw the post advertised in the Times Ed. It was in London and that suited me fine as my family and friends were there. I knew of the college before I went into teaching and remembered stating on my application form that being Black would help me to relate to the large Black student population there and allow them an opportunity to confidently share their experience of living in a White society. I also added that this whole situation did not exclude the White students as they would benefit from our experiences and we from their opinions and experiences of us. At the interview I suspected that they thought of me as a role model one that can motivate these students. I did not see myself so much as a role model but someone who maybe had the same or similar experiences to many of the Black students in that college. I was offered the job as a lecturer one and was eagerly anticipating the challenge.

When I started I was surprised to find the level of racism that existed in the staffroom. Not directed to me but to the Black students. In my presence discussions on students behaviour, complaints and problems were always about the Blacks. Card playing, loud music and so on. I can imagine what they said when I was not there. Now all staff knew that the White students got up to all sorts of things. They played cards, enjoyed loud music and were often to be found enjoying both with their Black friends. I felt I had to take a position either as a member of staff or as a Black person, defending something that I saw was right and a culture that I was used to. In any case the Black kids, though not angels, did not deserve the accusations they received. I said my piece and staff knew where I stood. After that I spent as little time as possible in the staffroom and very often in my free time I marked papers, prepared lessons or spent some time with some of my colleagues.

There were other problems in this staffroom. The engineering and technical staff formed a definite section within college. Their attitudes and behaviour were very different from other staff, especially those who taught liberal studies. Though an engineer my views were closly related to the liberal studies people. The engineers were aware of this and as you may know as a fraternity they demand loyalty and discipline. This caused many strained moments, though never open hostility. They accepted me as a skilled person and indicated that my academic qualifications or leanings did not count. In fact they were surprised at my level of education when I first arrived as most of them were very good tradesmen and skilled people who never took to academic work or membership of professional bodies other than trade unions. They sometimes asked me where I learnt my skills and were surprised that such things were taught in the West Indies.

Relationships in my classroom were very good as both Black and White students reacted in a positive way to my expectations. I think a White teacher in the same situation may not have had the same expectations, especially of the Black students. Some White students did show their surprise that I was bright enough to teach them especially in workshop skills and practice. I gained their respect for this and could possibly have created a basis for the Black students to believe in themselves. I also had the feeling that the students saw me as oppressed as they were, and their closeness to me was one way of giving me their support. While teaching I started an O.U. course which lasted for two years. I did the foundation course in technology and maths in an effort to get my first degree.

At that stage it was pretty tough going and an opportunity to go to Nigeria and teach attracted me. I decided to pack it all in here and go to Nigeria.

I spent six years in northern Nigeria and while there I was placed in jobs which I never thought I would get the opportunity to do. I would never have applied for such jobs in England. I was Head of Department in a technical college and then a Polytechnic. I performed all the duties of organising, planning and supervision quite adequately; and was praised by my principal who came from England. The educational value of my experience in Nigeria tells me that the fact that I cannot get that sort of job in England has nothing to do with my ability, but to do with the structure of the society. They could not see me, a Black person in such a job and psychologically made me think that as a Black person I could not see myself in such a job. My experience in Nigeria was of personal development. I saw myself a different person; a person with far more ability than the people in this society will have me believe. While in Nigeria I again thought of taking a degree course. I applied and was offered a one year bursary for teachers overseas through the Overseas Development Dept. The offer was designed for teachers coming back into the English system to keep up with recent developments in their field or any other they may wish to go into. I enrolled for the post-graduate Diploma in education at Manchester University department of adult and higher education, and got in on the strength of my H.N.C. Cert. Ed. and teaching experience. I was successful in this course and recommended to go forward to the M.Ed.programme. In this my tutor was very helpful and it made a big difference to my life at University. The encouraging atmosphere that exists in the department was also a feature of my time at the university, including my time on the M.Ed. programme. On this programme I met many people who had the same struggles as myself, especially people from overseas. We related well and helped each other by discussion and exchange of notes, books and so on. Those members of staff who selected the students needs to be congratulated for bringing together different peoples from different parts of the world to work together. I found the mixture an education in itself. Mind you, I was surprised that there weren't any Black lecturers about the university, especially with so many overseas students.

I came into the education system in England from a

workshop environment. I therefore feel that I came in as a member of the working class. I figure that any comments I have to make about the education system may be true for many working class people in this country. However, being an immigrant, a Black immigrant, there are other factors that I experienced and ones they are less likely to be part of. The problem of advice and concepts. The taken for granted view of the Black person and expectations, counselling and so on. Education does not totally suffice the needs of Black people as it is presently organised. Had I more information my situation could be very different. What little success I've got is due more to my motivation than any aspect of education. Of course education does count, but in England it is more likely to dissuade than persuade a person to do well.

Having achieved my M.Ed. I now want to go back to the West Indies and teach there. I want to give something back to the community that gave me my start. Also, I think me and my work will be better appreciated there.

He became somewhat disillusioned but this was partly
relieved when he was accepted on a further course largely
on the strength of his commitment to study. This gesture
of confidence in him and his ability to cope was the sort
of encouragement he needed. Mr Carter reports this period
in his life as very stressful, but he was determined to
continue. Accompanying this situation was the fact that
evening study was restrictive of wider personal
development, either in terms of forging meaningful
relationships with tutors, or participation in student
life. A further problem he encountered was that tutors
took it for granted that anyone allowed on a course had an
understanding of what was required of them and a matching
ability on formation of ideas. He saw this problem as
common among students regardless of racial background, but
felt that such a link was often made where Black students
are concerned. This, he feels, influenced the teaching of
such students and their performances.

The lack of course information and advice on further and higher education in England affected his career.

Employment and experience as a lecturer in further education exposed institutional racism. He was however able to mount and maintain fruitful relationships with all his students.

He recognises his background experience to be similar in many ways to other members of the defined working class.

The strong desire to return to his native community to work was realised in 1983.

CASE HISTORY 26 : EUGENE LEE

Born and educated in England, Mr Lee's parents came from the Caribbean. Now twenty years of age, he left school at sixteen and held various unskilled jobs. At present he is a voluntary youth worker with I.L.E.A., and is interested in possible training in this field. The young people who visit the club where he is employed are his peers, and his experience is intertwined with, and reflects their situation. This shared experience is extended to other members of the Black community, as he sees it.

GENERALLY AT SCHOOL there were only a few teachers I had any racial hassles with. Like the rest of the youths at the club, most of the teachers wasn't openly that way and were O.K. with us. I went to Archway Secondary which is comprehensive and have a lot of Black students; most as far as I know, born in this country. In that school when

the Black student reaches fifth form they are encouraged to
leave. I was encouraged to leave but had to wait till
Easter as that was the earliest leaving stage for me. It
was only one or two Black students who stay on in the sixth
form. Most of them staying on is White, even though you
will find as many Blacks in that school. Them discouraged
the Black student even if he wanted to try. Them would say
'No, you are not good enough'. But them are on the ones
who had the chance to make us good enough, and we get all
the blame. I don't know if it was school policy or not,
but I think so. I think that in school, myself and the
other youths, us born and growing up in this country,
should be given more information on what we could do and
what jobs we could get with what we done. They should also
give us more information about our culture and how the
system of politics really operates in this country,
especially local politics.

Education as such, as far as helping people, people
like me, has this thing about Black people. I saw it in
the attitude at school. Them think Black people are
dunces, we can't achieve things. To me, us Black youths
have a lot of sense and could learn things. It is how they
teach that turned me off and also a lot of the others. You
could see the teachers couldn't be bothered, they just want
you to be quiet. I went to school for eleven years of my
life and come out with nothing. The youths, like me are no
better off now. What can they do except go on the dole? I
reckon it is down to the people who run the educational
system to find out why this is happening, and to do
something about it. To me, further education for most of
us is no point. I won't mind some training for youth work,
but even for me it's too late. I will have to start from
the beginning. School did not work for me then, I couldn't
see it working now.

We look around now and see things our White
counterparts have and would like some of those things. A
job, money, clothes, a place to live. All those things.
If there is no work to get it then other means must be
found. Black people ain't dunces you know, but we are not
really given a real chance. The education system is set up
to prevent Black people from doing well in any large
numbers, so they could be better off. The youths and them
hold their heads when they see what their parents are going
through and what they have to go through. They don't want

to study, them already spent eleven years and get nothing out of it, why should they want more? They want to earn. Them that go back to college are put on dead end courses, just to get the numbers in college and people off the dole. After the course, they are no better off. There's a whole heap of institutions set up like the Adult Institute, right? and different Boroughs run different courses like numeracy, literacy, and so on. I am not interested in that. It should have been done in school, no wonder we are disillusioned. I myself am not quite sure how to help the Black youngsters, especially those at this club. We tried many things but we find they are not interested if it's not going to benefit them right away. Not six months, or a year later, but immediately. I understand how they feel because before I started to do this job I used to feel that way too. What they need is jobs. They have to live and a lot of them got families to look after, so anything geared to benefit them they would be interested in.

We are aware of people, White people wanting to use us for political causes. Some come around saying they want our vote and support, saying they are trying to do this and that and when I really check it out, nothing comes about, nothing beneficial, only talk. They can't fool the youth again, them wise. All the things like projects they are setting up mean nothing. They are not offering anything worthwhile. We are not stupid, we have common sense and some of us would rather go outside and hustle or thieve or whatever and get a living. Society let us down, that's how I see it. People talk a lot about training, and setting up small business. Workshops at youth centres are a waste of time, because there is no work afterwards and so many small businesses are shutting down.

The Government could set up real courses with real training, not the Y.T.S. rip off, and that will be a start because we are ambitious. We want to make something of our life, we don't want to live off the dole, and we don't want to be conned. As I see it, there are two sets of young Black people. Some may not want to make headway, but all I know, want to. Education failed both groups and we are all disillusioned with everyone and everything. Nobody is really interested. Many young Blacks are keen to learn a trade, but nothing doing. Some of them walk around for days and when they do get asked to go for an interview, the boss always say 'We'll let you know' but them never do.

The only help that is happening is some funds for special projects from the local Labour Party. If it's Tory you can't get it, and some Labour councils may be stopped from giving it by the Conservative Government. If this happens it would cause a lot of problems at street level and that is why they are giving the police more powers.

They are getting ready. At the moment whenever there is an arrest of a Black youth and them come for you, they block off the whole area with dozens of policemen and vans, for one Black youth. It is like if the youth is the biggest criminal, a murderer or something. Even when the police can't find anything like drugs, they find some reason to assault us. If we complain or show any resistance, they lock us up and give an injection to control the person they arrest. Them view is that the young Black is too disruptive. People may not believe this is true, especially people living out of London and if they are White, but believe me it is happening in London every day. The government's not interested, teachers are not interested. Things are getting worse and they are all just looking on. Anyone with common sense could see that the rich man is getting richer and the poor man suffering more. The Black man is poor and the government want to keep us there. Look how many Black kids leave school and have nothing, no future, no culture, nothing to hold them together. That is why they are running wild.

People, including parents ask why we youths go on so? Them know the reason but they don't want to accept it. I can't see things getting better. One of the problems we face even at this centre is to get the youths, them interested in Black history. After a couple of weeks they just drop it. You see they have to cope with too much pressure to bother with history. They hear people talking about slavery this and slavery that, but they ain't seen on one come forward and do something about it. They hear a whole heap of talk about living in a ghetto, poverty, slavery and all that, and we are still here today. So they are not interested in history, education and them things. What they are interested in is about now, they are not that interested in the past. They ask what can you do for us now? How can that help me in this situation with a lot of problems? Because of all the problems, some Black people is kinda freaking out. Them trying to get the pressure off their mind right? The doctor who come for us will say 'He is mad' and threw him in a madhouse. But it is not madness, the man is only trying to free himself from the problems, 'cos it's like saying that him is a bird and that's how he see it, right? He just keep coming up against obstacles and barriers, right? I've seen it. As soon as you break through one barrier a next one is there, then regulations to keep us down. When the Black youths are given a good education, and real opportunity to better themselves, then we could talk about history and that. The Black youth see everyone making it except him; all the Whites who went to school with him got something. He checks it out and blames himself for not making it. His brother who is in the same situation can't help him. He say, Cha, even my own Black brother is against me and that cause more pressure. What have education done, what can it do? You know, Black girls, them are even worse off. They don't go mad to the same extent but it is very difficult for them to get any independence. They come to the centre every day. They get no jobs and them got 'O' levels and that. The trend is to have a baby so they can get a flat and family allowance. They have less of a future than the Black youths. They often stay home and get bored, with nothing to do but children to look after. That's no life, them life wash up. But still the Black woman blames the Black men for not getting a job, they can't see that it is not his fault. The girls and society will have to understand, that at street level when we go out looking for work we often get stopped by the police, yes, in broad daylight. I already explain how they behave. The next thing them try to do is to nail some charge on us and that means no one will employ us. They are hoping that by keeping us down we will get fed up and ask for money to go to the West Indies. But the youths who were born here, here is home. They have relatives there like Poles in England have in Poland; but this is home. The youths can't understand why the White people treat us so, why them alienate us? Even the police who arrest us used to go to school with us.

The form of racism through encouragement to leave school at the earliest possible time was a common experience for most Black children in that school; as was the lack of motivation they received from the learning situation that existed. The view that eleven years of schooling was only preparation for unemployment and receiving social welfare is representative of this group's feelings.

It would surprise the outsider to learn how much Eugene and members of this group despise the idea of being on the dole. Eugene's statement is indicative of their feelings. 'Day by day, week by week, we have nothing to look forward to, we've nothing. We sleep more; get up and all we look forward to is this little giro. A few days later it's gone and we have to wait till next week for another little giro. And so life goes on, there is no future'. Their need for useful paid work and marketable skills training is stated time and again during the interview. Disillusion turns to self-blame and disgust. It sometimes creates uneasy relationships between members of the community.

Mr. Lee found schooling 'a turn-off' and of no value later on except to prepare the young Black person to collect social benefits.

The absence of meaningful occupation is seen by Mr. Lee as central to the experience of the young Black person.

The situation of Black girls is seen as urgent.

Mr. Lee believes that through their combined action the government and the rest of White British society hopes to induce the Black youth to leave these shores.

CASE HISTORY 27 : TERRY HICKS

Mr Hick's educational experience occurs for the greater part in London. His parents are of West Indian origin and his only experience of their homeland is from a brief holiday spent there. The visit was a good learning experience comparing attitudes to life there and in England. This visit however served to strengthen his belief that Britain is home. A youth worker, Mr Hicks found that school ill prepared him for post-school life.

MY TIME AT school did not mean much to me. On leaving to get a job I found that the stuff I learnt at school was no use to help me get anything. At school it was either the students were good enough to get a couple of 'O' levels, or hard luck. No kind of education existed where you could use your hands. A lot of people can do practical things but they haven't got qualifications like 'O' levels, and that means they are not given the chance to do something with their hands. To me 'look and learn' is better than 'O' levels in certain types of jobs, like for example, woodwork. At school that sort of thing was presented as diagrams to work from, but most of the time I could not really understand it. The teacher was not patient either and never bothered to explain how to work from the diagrams.

After I left school I went to a youth club, and started to learn woodwork in this little place attached to the club. I found learning this way was interesting and useful and completely different to anything at school. I really enjoyed it. At school, because I couldn't understand it, I did not enjoy it. It had no meaning to me. I used to get really fed up with it. I used to think why are they showing me those diagrams all the time? I would've preferred the teacher starting off the class by showing us how to actually make a table or something. It was nothing like that, just diagrams showing parts of furniture. These diagrams were given to us while the teacher went off to do something else.

I suppose primary school was alright, because we concentrated on the basic skills and the teacher explained everything well and told us why we had to do it. In secondary school the teachers always showed Black people in a negative way and this gave the White kids the idea that Blacks were inferior especially when we did history lessons. It was only after I left school I realised this. They never showed us anything positive about the Black man's history, even though there were many Black students in the school. It was a mixed school and classes were divided into streams. I was in one class that had some bright people and though I coped well I wasn't too happy. I was the only Black pupil in that class. I did not take any C.S.E's or 'O' levels while at school, as deep down I did not see the point. I knew youths who had 'O' and 'A' levels and could not get work. I left school as soon as I could which was at Easter time, and I can't say that the teachers encouraged me to stay. I had nothing to go to when I left as the careers teacher did not give me any ideas on what sort of things were available. She never really helped much. She used to ask us what we wanted to be, and if you said you wanted to be a fireman or something like that she would write it down and that was that, we got

no further. It seemed that they were not really interested
in placing us but had to keep the records straight. She
was not unusual, because most of the teachers were not
interested in us. They never bothered to get any of us
Blacks interested. If we did well and get on top of the
group, it was mainly because of our own efforts. Half the
time the teachers used to get fed up, though some of them
used to start off fairly keen. If a student didn't care
they would not bother any more.

    I've had several jobs since leaving school, and none
of them was to do with what I was taught at school. My
first job was making springs and I have also done some spot
welding and worked with community industry. Most of the
guys at community industry were in trouble with the police,
though I myself was not. When we got to the community
industry base we were sent to peoples' houses to paint and
decorate and so on. No college type training was involved,
and it helped me to develop my skills in plastering and
painting. This was great; they did not ask for any 'O' or
'A' levels, they just let me get on with it, with an
instructor giving me tips. I left that job for this one,
working as a youth worker. It is something I always wanted
to do and took this chance when it came up. This present
scheme (youth centre) started from a similar scheme we had
going but it was not so well organised. In that first
scheme the police used to visit us often, sometimes
smashing the place up. We got fed up of this and went to
the law centre for help and advice. They helped us set up
this place with money from the local authority. They also
informed us of our legal situation and so on. The police
know this and they have generally kept away, though when
they do come they are careful how they treat us.

    In this centre everyone is urged to suggest ways on
how we want to run things. This is to show that we can run
things and are willing to take part in working in England;
if they will accept us and give us an opportunity to show
what we can do. Most of the youths in the centre are
unemployed and have been for some time. Their chances of
getting a job are really slim as many places ask for
qualifications like G.C.E.'s and that. What most of the
youths want is training in something practical. People say
we don't want to work because they offer us jobs that we
can't take because we have no qualifications. I know if we
had qualifications they would not make that offer. It is

only made because they know the score. I've worked with people who have G.C.E's and find that when it comes down to real grafting they don't know a thing.

Most of the youths who come here have given up hope because they're a bit cheesed off. Some have tried these youth opportunities schemes, but that is a waste of time. What the youths want is a real job with a real wage. Generally most of them see going back into education as a waste of time. They've already had enough of that experience and those who want to, feel that it must be done in a way where Black teachers will be very involved. I feel that we are exploited by the White teachers who are not really interested in seeing Blacks do well. I think most White teachers are only in it for the money, at least those I have come across. The youths have checked education like this. They went to school and it never got them no where. So what is there to do to be something in life? I think the cause of so many Black youths failing at school is because of the way the teachers teach. Very often it is difficult to understand what they are on about, but when you get a teacher who could explain his stuff then the students will learn. I found that with maths.

The future is just one of drifting. We have one guy who comes here and who has seven 'O' levels, the only job he could get was in a bingo hall collecting tickets. Imagine, with all those qualifications. In London there is also a lot of hassle with the police against Black youth. Very often we are picked up for nothing, and the public think we are making it up. We see it, live it; it happens to us. It is our experience and it is real. Des, my mate, was stopped and searched on his way home the other day. He just came from work and they stopped him. It took some White people to tell the police to leave the youth as he wasn't doing anything wrong. They saw everything and because they were White he was allowed to go. By that time they had insulted him and roughed him up.

Education is useful but it is no use if you have ignorant teachers, police and employers. It is only useful if we Blacks can get the chance to use it afterwards.

Mr Hicks did point out the link between the police and school as one important aspect of the situation of Black youths in London. The police were often in school and sometimes invited to speak to the pupils. On other occasions they came as part of their investigations of deviant behaviour of some pupils. In both situations their attitude was the same: 'This is the law, break it or challenge it, and you're in for it'. Never any discussions, criticisms or points of information. Black youth seemed to be marked by the police who always got support from the school.

The voluntary formation of Mr. Hick's youth club aimed to demonstrate the youths' wish to participate in constructive work, and to avert possible confrontation with the police, who had actually smashed up their former club. Their new one was subject to extensive harassment by the police, who often gave weak explanations for entry. This led the group to seek legal advice and information and then set up the present centre, which so far has gained the support of the local authority and community, and witnessed a decrease in police interest. Mr Hicks was quick to add that this did not mean that the police had ceased their stop and search tactics (popularly known as S and S) of Black youth on the streets of London.

Mr Hicks feels that the quality of teaching, and lack of teacher commitment, are major factors in the failure of Blacks in the education system.

He found the unhelpful and uninspired attitude of the careers teachers to be typical of most staff in the school.

Mr Hicks sees the attitude of the police as an important factor in post-school life for Blacks in London.

Frustration and anger due to the lack of hope for the future describes the situation of the Black youth in London today.

Post-school education is not seen as presenting anything more relevant to their needs today than school education did in the past.

CASE HISTORY 28 : GERRY LANDSBERG

Mr. Landsberg was born in Zimbabwe (then Rhodesia) of German/African parentage. One of three brothers, he arrived in England in 1978 as a political refugee. The opportunity to leave Rhodesia then was also influenced by his desire to further his education. In Rhodesia he was designated coloured, and that influenced the type of schooling that was available to him. During discussions with another respondent it was suggested that the writer contact Mr. Landsberg and Mr. Matanda as both experienced the education systems of England and British colonial Africa. It was felt that the comparisons of systems might be useful to this study.

IN RHODESIA ALL education had to be paid for, unlike Britain where much of it is free. This meant that only those who could afford it would send their children to

school. I went to a mission school which was supposed to
be the best for non-Whites (coloureds). The education
system was run along apartheid lines, that is schools for
Whites, Coloureds and Blacks. For the millions of Black
people in Zimbabwe (then Rhodesia) there were only about
ten secondary schools where the student could take 'O' and
'A' levels. The system was designed to really educate only
a few and they were White. The others were educated to a
fashion despite the system. For the majority education
ended at the secondary stage after which most went into
semi-skilled and unskilled jobs. The few who were luckier,
and got 'O' and 'A' levels went into lower clerical and
teaching jobs. Never into professional and management
jobs.

The Whites who totalled about twelve thousand had over
one hundred secondary schools, the best teachers and
facilities. The Catholic mission schools used to say that
they were multiracial but no Whites would attend their
schools if Blacks were allowed in. For example, at St.
George's, which was run by the mission, they had over three
hundred student population and they allowed ten non- white
students; all of whom came from influential and
wealthy parentage. Entry into that school cost about £300
per term. All heads of schools and colleges were White
men, even in Black schools staffed for the most part by
Black teachers. Black teachers could never teach in a
White school.

An important point in my schooling was the history
lessons. We were not taught anything of our own country.
In Zimbabwe (then Rhodesia) there are two main tribes, the
Shona and Matabele, but Rhodesian history as we were told
started when the settlers came, conquered and set up the
state of Rhodesia. As a result the Blacks were made to
feel inferior. Recently, historical lessons of the country
talks about the struggles of the tribes in the face of the
colonial settlers, and gives the picture of resistance and
struggles, only lost because of the superior arms of the
settlers. The rest of our history lessons was of the
British Empire and England. The system was designed so
that Black people would grow up thinking that Great Britain
was the best, the masters of the world. I knew more about
England than most English kids, and very little about my
own country. English was the taught language with French
as the second language. It was only used in conversation

and passed on by family and the community.

I got nine 'O' levels at my secondary school and stayed on to do 'A' levels, with the hope of going on to university. The only university was the one in Rhodesia and the competition for places offered to non-Whites was fierce. As a result there were few Blacks at the university. The only answer for Blacks who arrive at the pre-university stage, was to study out of the country. This was not easy as there was a lot of hassle for Blacks to get passports. A number of us left the country to go to university overseas at a time when we were very much against the political regime of Ian Smith. My secondary schooling experience was similar to my primary, in that the same situation existed. There was no hostility as such by the White teachers to the Black students. We always looked up to them as our masters, and anything that was said, went. Now I look back and think how could I have tolerated all that. I wish I knew then what I know now.

Not surprisingly there was no such thing as a career advice, a career structure for Blacks was not considered. The only advice we got was from our parents or other members of the family or friends. There were careers advice centres but they were for Whites. Even Whites that were ignorant were guided towards industry and into apprenticeships. Once finished they became foremen over a Black labour force. We used to consider them as low Whites, but they were still our bosses. All they had to do was supervise as we did all the work.

After my 'A' levels I worked as a clerk in the education department (African division) and realising that my prospects for advancement was nil I decided to leave for England. I disliked the political system anyway so making a decision to leave was easy. The problem was that my pass did not allow me permission for a passport to go to Europe. The only place I could go to was Botswana. I felt once there, as a political refugee I would get a passport to England. I arrived at Heathrow and was detained for over ten hours being questioned by immigration officers. They threatened to deport me even though political refugees from Rhodesia were allowed in. M.P.'s like Andrew Faulds and a member of the Zimbabwe Refugee Association came down and fought my case and saw me through.

Once I was settled I got on to education. I contacted the office of the United Council for Overseas Student

Affairs, from information given me by the Zimbabwe Refugee Association. I also learnt that the Ministry of Overseas Development was giving grants to refugee students from Zimbabwe. I applied and was successful. The Ministry also supplied me with information for courses and guidelines for study. At this stage I was unsure of what subject I wanted to study and considered Business Study or Law. I was then advised by another Zimbabwian, also a student, to take something in the technical field. His view was that on gaining independence our country will need technical and skilled people as there were many non-technical Zimbabwian students about. I remembered that my uncle, a manufacturer of spectacles, was one of the only two such people in the country, that I know of. The other manufacturer was Black. As there were no other Blacks in that field of work I decided on it. I found out that there were only about four places in the U.K. doing opthalmic technicians courses, including City of London Polytechnic. I submitted an application and was accepted. At polytechnic there were a few Black students on the course, two of Indian origin and two of West Indian origin. Actually one of the Indian lads came from Uganda. The relationship between students were fairly amicable, though a small group of White students tended, now and then, to make racist remarks. The lecturers on the whole, if they were racists, hid it well. That is except the teacher who was in charge of the practical side of the course. I could see he did not like Blacks. He tried to hide it but it showed in the way he related and treated the Blacks. He would never spend the time or the effort advising Blacks like he did with the White students. Although some of the Black students were doing better work than the Whites he still favoured them. I came from a system where you get to recognise such attitudes and behaviour, so I was on the right lines as far as that teacher was concerned. His reaction may be in response to the fact that the presence of an intelligent Black person was not acceptable to his thinking. Probably he was a born racist. He behaved as if he was there to do a job for a salary and I felt that if he could choose his students we would not have been there. You see racism is a central part of this system too. You must remember that the British are the ones that instituted racism wherever they went. They were open racists and systems of education they set up reflected that racism.

The British education system to me is no different to the apartheid system in my country, as far as I saw it in college. It is hard for me to describe but I can feel it. I sense that it is geared on the aspirations of the White race. I cannot comment on primary and secondary schooling as I have not been part of that system here, but if my college experience is similar to what kids here get in school then the whole system is no different than at home, e.g. there seems to be recognition of the existence of other races.

> At this point in the interview two police officers interrupted the proceedings. (See notes at end.)

Where was I? Yes; the comparison is in the attitude of White people and their institutions. Discrimination, racism is a difficult thing to measure but it is experienced, believe me. I get that same sort of feeling where I work. How people approach me, how they talk to me and the things they say when they think I am out of earshot. They talk of equal opportunity, but in reality it does not exist. It is not much different in Rhodesia because even the police ask for identity. When I finished Polytechnic I could not get a job in my field to gain some experience. This job with the local authority came up and I decided to take this opportunity to get some experience in administration. My immediate boss wants me to stay, but now that my studies have finished and my country is independent I am expected to go back. I am anxious to return but would like this work experience first. I want to go back because I am sick and tired of the harassment I get by the police. Like what just happened to us. These situations are designed to humiliate us you know. My experience in Rhodesia tells me so.

A feature of this education system that interests me, and one we in Zimbabwe can learn from. In Zimbabwe (then Rhodesia) we had to compete for limited places at a cost. We had to get our 'O' and 'A' levels while at school. If for instance I did not make it then that was it for the rest of my life, as there was no way of re-entering the education system. Adult education in England as I see it gives people another chance, a chance to return at a later stage, and that is a great idea. Also I think it's good to

have careers advice and to have at the students disposal
all those facilities. All those things are really good, it
is the people, the racism that gets me down. Another
similarity with Rhodesia is the percentage of
representation of Black people in this borough. The count
of ethnic minorities is forty eight per cent but if you
observe the Black representation in this borough it is
nearer two per cent. Yet most of the politicians come in
on an ethnic vote. The representation is similar in the
education sector, taking teachers, administrators and so
on. The ethnic minorities pay forty eight per cent of the
rates, but do they have anywhere near forty eight per cent
representation? No. Black people should insist on their
right, and the authority should be made to reflect its
community. This situation could change with education. In
Zimbabwe education was seen as both a colonising tool, and
also a tool of liberation. Armed struggle was necessary
but education was always a part of that struggle.
Education must have some meaning, some way to show that it
will bring about change. It is only then it will be
useful. Maybe this is the idea behind adult education in
this country? I do not know.

Note; This interview took place in a car park inside the
writer's car. It was a hot sunny day and no other quiet,
convenient place could be found. Facilities at Mr
Landsberg's work place were not available; many other
people were lunching in their cars in the park.

The two police officers, both from the Harringey force,
approached the car with a dog. They asked what we were
doing and when told, they asked many questions and demanded
identification. On production of identification officer 68
looked surprised that the writer could be linked to a
university. Having satisfied their request for identity
they said they were checking as cars have been stolen from
the park. The writer enquired as to why other occupants in
the park were not challenged. No reply was given. Both
interviewer and interviewee felt that in our case the link
between race and crime was made by the officers.

Intrusion by the police during the interview may be the subject of many interpretations by those who come across this piece. The interviewee saw it as a justification for his claim of continued police harassment, no different from the attitude of the police in Rhodesia. To the writer it was an anxious moment; a new and frightening experience, only heard to have happened to other people. The event, and the manner in which both of us were confronted, while others were ignored may be indicative of the way Blacks are perceived and labelled by the police.

Mr. Landsberg's comparison shows that while Rhodesia is overtly racist, an attitude manifest in its system of apartheid, Britain is covertly apartheid. He noted the problems that arise when one tries to measure attitudes that are covertly expressed. But having observed the actions and behaviour of people he has encountered in Britain, he was able to suggest specific areas of comparison where race was the predominant factor.

To him, apartheid in Britain does exist and can be witnessed in the classroom in the organisation of the work place and in community representation.

The preparation of Blacks through education to fill the ranks of the proletariat is for him similar to the Rhodesian system. There was however, no pretence in Rhodesia that 'equality' was part of their thinking. The under representation of different ethnic groups in managing the affairs of the community bears a striking resemblance in both societies.

Continuing education was seen as the one positive aspect of the British educational system that the newly independent Zimbabwe will take on board. It is this sector, according to Mr Landsberg, that is likely to initiate strategies for change in both societies.

He feels that Britain does not offer him a fair chance in life. He is hoping to return to Zimbabwe.

The absence of ethnic representation and police harassment are reminiscent of Rhodesia.

Adult education and its attendant structures are a positive educational facility in England.

Education for colonisation could be re-structured to become education for liberation.

CASE HISTORY 29 : FRANCIS MATANDWA

Born in Zimbabwe (then Rhodesia) of African parentage, Francis is one of eight children. His father is a teacher, his mother a housewife. Francis arrived in England in 1975 with the intention of studying and hoping that his status as a political refugee would not hinder his plans. He is at present a teacher in London.

THE EDUCATION SYSTEM in Rhodesia was divided into three major sections, European, Coloured/Indian and African. It is a system similar to that in South Africa. Most of the schools in Rhodesia were run by missionaries; schooling had to be paid for and there were none in the outlying country districts. This meant that the African child's chances of getting any education were influenced by all those factors and more. It shows too that the system was not designed with the Blacks in mind, but simply to

202 HOPES, FRUSTRATIONS, ACHIEVEMENTS

make literate sufficient numbers of us so that we could work competently for them.

I was born and brought up in Harare, one of the major cities in Rhodesia. My father was a teacher and as a salaried person he was able to afford to send us to school. My primary schooling was in a state school, and was enjoyable as we were involved in many activities. At that age we grew up accepting the system of virtual apartheid as that was how we thought it ought to be. From that school I went to a Catholic secondary school run by Jesuits. There I did my 'O' and 'A' levels, hoping to go on to the University of Rhodesia. I later found out that grants to university were only given to Black students if they were going there to train as teachers. If I wanted to take a degree in anything other than teacher education I was not eligible for a grant. I was unsure whether I wanted to be a teacher or not and the only alternative for further study was to go abroad. After my 'A' levels I got a job with the Ministry of Education as a clerk. I took this to give me some time to think of my next step. I found it increasingly difficult to come to terms with the political regime of Ian Smith and the system of apartheid, which by now I was well aware of; and unwilling to accept.

In the ministry I found my White counterparts with less qualifications were my supervisors and even the White filing clerks who were females got higher wages than more experienced Black staff. Some of them had only 'O' levels, sometimes none. They certainly had no 'A' levels. That sort of situation angered me. At that time the war was going on and people in civil service jobs were being conscripted into the army. It was a very difficult time as I could not see myself fighting for the Smith regime against my own people. I was violently against the idea and there was no other alternative but to try and leave the country. I write to a friend who was a teacher in England, but came from Rhodesia. He sent me the address and information of a college of education in England, I applied and was offered a place. I then resigned my job and experienced the hassle of trying to get a passport to leave the country. Because of contacts I was able to get one and arrived in England in May 1975. I informed the immigration authorities that I came as a student fleeing from the Smith regime. I was advised by the authorities to get a valid passport as soon as possible.

I later chose not to go to the college of education where I had a place as I found out that the college was very far from the people I knew. My people lived in London, and this place was up north. I did not want to be on my own in a strange country. I later applied to a college in Tottenham to do Accountancy and stayed there for a year. I coped well but found the course dry and uninteresting. I then applied to the Polytechnic of North London to study the Humanities; a B.A. in English and History. I was the only Black student on this Poly course and found all the other students had come straight from schools and were quite naive about what was happening around them. Our relationship as students were good and pretty amicable with the teachers. One view of the Poly was that it was a fairly progressive and radical place producing people like Tariq Ali. The other view was of its link with racism through the director at that time. It was well known that the director was the Principal at the University of Rhodesia and actually collaborated with the Smith regime. There were vigorous student protests and many staff supported us. While most of the students and staff that I came in touch with were alright some members of the staff knowingly supported racist activities. The students felt that as the Principal influenced college policy no radical change could take place while he and certain staff were about. There was a move to replace him. The rest of the three years at the Poly were rewarding but uneventful.

I had no special plans to teach after I completed my degree, as I was unsure about careers, but saw an article in the Times about teaching in Harringey. The article stated that one in twenty five children in Harringey schools were Black and only one in seven hundred teachers were Black. The authority were recruiting people from Black and other ethnic groups who were suitably qualified to train as teachers. There I was with an Honours degree, unsure of what to do so I applied for a grant for teacher training and got a letter refusing my application; on the grounds that I was not a resident in the U.K. While awaiting their response I wrote off and was accepted to do the B.G.C.E. at St. Mary's Institute of Education. Due to Harringey's response I contacted my local M.P. on the grounds that I was a citizen of the U.K. and colonies and should get a grant. The M.P. fought my case and I was

awarded a grant to study at St. Mary's. At St. Mary's I
enroled to take the option in Multi-cultural education but
found the course good, while the option did not relate to
known experience in the ethnic minority community. As
students we discovered that the lecturers had not been
inside a school for fifteen to twenty years, and as far as
we were able to establish they had no contact or experience
of the ethnic communities. The lessons took the form and
content of material drawn from aspects of comparative
religion. Nothing about racism, politics, history or
culture. We requested outside speakers from the community
and were really impressed when this Black woman who worked
with the I.L.E.A. multi ethnic unit came to speak to us.
She was really good, relating the school experience of
teachers and kids to race. A good mix of reality and
theory, not as before totally in the abstract and unrelated
to peoples' experience. I was surprised that the college
did not employ members of the ethnic community to make
departmental contributions.

After receiving my B.G.C.E. I thought it would be
fairly easy to get a job especially as my teaching practice
went well and that Harringey wanted Black teachers. I
applied for a number of jobs always attaching a picture of
myself with the view that they will be looking for Black
teachers. I never got one interview. It seems that very
often local education authorities make statements for
public relations and consumption, but do not really mean to
carry out those ideas. I went to the education offices of
the local authority for some explanation and they told me
not to be worried, asking me to put myself forward for
supply teaching. I did and for the next few weeks I heard
nothing. It was also coming to the beginning of the school
year and I was really worried that I would not get a job.
As it happened, I heard of this job at a local school. I
went down to see the head and got the job on a one year
temporary contract. All that time I heard nothing from
Harringey.

I started at this school and quickly got into knowing
my students. I related to them very well, though they
found it strange that I taught English when some of their
parents who were English could not speak nor write
properly. 'How could you teach English. You are an
African and my parents who are English do not speak
proper ' this lad asked. I found that the students related

more to my accent than my race. The staff relationship
with me tended to be more of a patronising nature, though
some have made statements that smack of extreme racism.
However, I quickly put a stop to such statements from
people like that. After my year there I applied for and
got another teaching post. It was quite an interesting one
working in a unit for disturbed kids. I suspect the reason
why they took me was that most of the kids at the unit were
Black, and the worse behaved of the White kids. It may be
that the kids could not relate to the White middle class
teachers who were there. The head must have felt that a
Black teacher could be useful in such a situation. I later
discovered the other teachers refused to cover my class
while I was away, because of their behaviour. I understand
from the kids that they were actually told to stay away or
they were packed off to a room and told to get on with it.
I had the feeling that I was not paid to educate the kids
but to keep them off the streets; in a sense both the kids
and I felt the system had rejected them.

Due to cutbacks I was made redundant, at least that is
what I was told, though I had my doubts. The head told me
that there was a job in another school in the area and it
would be in my own interest if I took it. I went along to
see the head and got this temporary post to start right
away. The prospects don't look too good and the chance of
promotion is virtually nil. I find that looking around me
and from my own experience Black teachers in the system
experience two things. First we are unlikely to get
promotion even when we are qualified for it, and secondly,
we tend to be given the difficult classes, not 'O' or 'A'
level which we are qualified to teach. Because, like in
Rhodesia, we are not given opportunities for responsible
positions it is difficult to introduce the teaching of
ethnic history and culture in schools and colleges. I know
the I.L.E.A. has a policy on this, but it is necessary to
work inside schools to get things done. It's a method I
find quite useful. There is another point to make; that
is, the politicians talk about having more Black teachers
and multi-cultural material for schools. But some heads
who choose teachers and plan syllabus are not even keen to
de-segregate their staffroom. It may be due to staff
pressure and some people may be surprised to learn that
segregation in an underhanded way takes place in some of
the staffrooms that I have been in. This is reminiscent of

the schools for Blacks in Rhodesia where the White staff keep themselves separate from Black staff.

An amusing side to my career so far is that I find that whenever the inspector of V.I.P.'s visit the schools, the head shows me off and calls me by my first name. I am sure this is to show the head as a progressive person. The interesting thing is that he still gives me special classes and not G.C.E. work. I feel this affects my future in the profession as any new employer will only see me as someone who can teach remedial classes.

That he is allowed to teach in a school with White children shows a significant difference in the two communities, though he is aware that if some teachers and administrators had their way, that freedom would be curtailed. Evidence that such an attitude exists emerges from confrontations with White colleagues and his observations of lines of demarcation in some staffrooms.

In Rhodesia, the White hierarchy often selected members of the Black ethnic community to be paraded as representatives of their community, using such instances to display their support for democratic principles. Mr. Matandwa's experience finds a similar development in headmasters who are eager to be seen as sympathetic towards racial equality. To him such behaviour is a mechanism, to disguise their true attitudes.

His students' fascination for his teaching of English is more apparent in their relations with him than any reaction to his race.

He experienced a patronising attitude from staff which he thought fitted in well with the covert segregation practiced in some staffrooms.

CASE HISTORY 30 : PETER

I AM ONE of eight children of Afro-Caribbean origin
born in the West Indies. My father was a taxi driver, and
hill farmer, and my mother took in other people's washing
and ironing. Poverty was not uncommon in our community so
my life style was not seen as strange. Those who enjoyed a
better standard of living did not interpret their good
fortune in terms of a higher status. At that stage in my
life racism was not part of my reality. In our village
there were few White families, all at some point in their
family history had married locally. Whites who I came
later to recognise as the owning class lived in areas
exclusively theirs and well away from our community. The
fact that my Godfather was of German origin, the son of the
manager and engineer of the local pumping station and my
Godmother was of Spanish origin, gives a view of the
community. Both were White and accepted as members of the
Community.

What we tended to have in Trinidad in those days could

be interpreted as ethnicism, as there was little interracial marriage. However, when it did occur there was not
the conflict, frustration and pressures that attend similar
situations in England. Over the centuries some
intermarriage took place, and though not always encouraged,
it was not despised. The different ethnic and racial
groups are respected for wanting to maintain their culture
and tradition; but all adhere to a strong national
identity.

I attended school to fourteen years of age. I took my
college entrance exam, passed but was unable to win a
bursary, and knew that my parents could not afford to send
me. I remember being very sad looking at my friends going
off to college on the morning bus. I secretly cried and
that episode might have been when I decided to do something
in education. I felt I had to prove 'them' wrong, though I
did not really know who 'they' were. I did not blame my
parents nor my teachers but I felt I had to be successful.
There were few apprenticeships at that time available to
boys from the country districts, so training of that type
did not come into any discussion at all. In fact, of my
peer group numbering forty or so, only three went on to
some form of apprenticeship training, one in forestry,
another at the telephone company and one at the electricity
board. It was normal for those boys and girls who did not
go off to school to get jobs through relatives or from
friends. My parents knew of this gentleman who was a
handyman and sent me off with him on a sort of
apprenticeship. After a year with him and through his
contact I got a job as a delivery boy in a drug store
(chemist in this country). I stayed in this job for a
couple of years and again through contact got a more
prestigious job as a clerk at the radio station. I worked
there for about eight years attempting at all times to
obtain a more secure post, only to get as far as a studio
control operator. While employed at the radio station I
tried to get on to part-time evening classes at the local
college, but was refused entry as I did not have a history
of academic success. That refusal really hurt me. I still
feel upset at that treatment as I knew I could have done
fairly well. My other learning option was to attend non-
vocational classes in community work. This did not lead
anywhere but it means I was doing something and likely to
meet the sort of people that could help me. I attended

these classes every Wednesday night, seven to nine p.m. for two years.

I also realised while at the radio station that prospects for promotion were not too bright and by a twist of fate my best friends decided to sail to England. There is a general feeling that if anyone wanted to do well they would go off to England to study. Both my friends had training occupations awaiting them, one in psychiatric nursing, the other with the R.A.F. I decided to leave with them as this was my big opportunity to be qualified in something. I had no money and the family was unable to help me. I scraped, borrowed and saved for six months and got the minimum together. I had no family contacts in the U.K. and though there were no problems of entry into the U.K. then, it was not easy to settle in. I had no idea of how to enter the education system and even where to go for guidance or how to gain information to obtain such guidance. When I left the radio station back home they gave me letters of reference to submit to the parent company to get a job if I so wished. I did that and was employed first as a messenger in their administrative department and then as a labourer in their repairs department. I asked for a move to the repairs section as the pay was higher and I needed the money to pay off debts back home. For the first two weeks I stayed at my friends' relatives and by chance met this Jewish couple who gave me lodgings, 'digs' in their house.

My first impression of England was not the weather nor queues, but that there were poor Whites, beggars. There were Whites who were not very bright, and some lived in conditions which for Whites would not be believed back home. There, Whites are the elite and have all the advantages of elitism. Here, I was faced with the stunning revelation that there were many White folk who were not highly qualified. The assistant chief engineer at the radio station back home was an English expatriate who had O.N.D. qualifications and the style of life befitting senior technical personnel overseas. I was later surprised to learn the value of the O.N.D. qualification in England.

On transferring to the repairs department I noticed on my way to and from work a sign that said 'Working Men's College', this was in Mornington Crescent near Camden Town, London. The small notice board advertised that G.C.E. subjects were taught there. There I was, similar to someone dying of thirst in the desert lying under a cactus plant.   I had no idea of how to get into the education system and yet, it was all around me.   I went in, enquired, and enrolled to take English, Maths and Logic over two years at 'O' level.   I chose logic because I did not know what it was and I wanted another 'O' level.   I quite enjoyed logic, much more than Maths or English.   I then went on to take three 'A' levels at the North Western Polytechnic in Kentish Town, again over a two year period at evening class.   I found part-time study very, very hard, especially during the winter time.   I started work at 7.3o a.m. and finished at 5.30 p.m. and had one hour break before setting off to evening class.   Monday, Wednesday and Thursday I attended classes.   Tuesday and Friday I prepared homework.   I took Economics, Economic History and Politics at 'A' level and remember the Politics tutor Mr F.W.G. Benemy who wrote **Whitehall - Town Hall.**   He was very constructive and helpful to me.

I had no idea how to move into higher education having been successful at 'A' levels.   The Polytechnic had no careers person available, so I had to go. about blindly searching for this point of entry.   I wrote off to London University but when I did not hear from them it was too late for university entry that year.   They sent me a list of Polytechnics and advised me to write off to one that did their degree externally.   I contacted Manchester Polytechnic because I understood from a friend that it was less expensive to live in Manchester.   I registered for the B.Sc. in Sociology and spent three years there with mixed emotions.   I had no knowledge of how to handle concepts and play around with ideas.   I did not know how to learn and I had no background knowledge of what the tutors expected. Tutors seem to take it for granted that a person with 'O' levels will understand degree level work.   This belief was a central influence on my academic performance.   Had I some introduction to degree study I would not have experienced the anxieties and frustrations that visited me.

Racism was the other factor to influence my academic life in higher education (first degree study).   In my then naive state I never expected educated folk to be racist. The lecturer in Psychology was blatantly racist, and this was known by all staff and students in the department. Quite often his comments to me and the only other Black student on the course were extremely rude and hateful, but neither of us knew how to handle the situation, there was nobody to refer to, to remedy the situation. I had no reference point with which to oppose this tutor. I could not respond with evidence from text nor from any other credible source. Though at times I felt I wanted to destroy him physically I leaned towards proving that I was academically capable and could disprove the basis of his ideas. This circumstance scared me. It is however useful to note that the seven other tutors in the department were unlike that tutor, especially the survey methods and statistics tutor who was very responsive to our needs.

After my degree studies I had no idea what to do. The Polytechnic did not have its own careers service and I was advised to use the facilities at the university. The careers advisers there were not very helpful and advised on either clerical work in the civil service, the forces, social work or teaching. I chose teaching and was advised to take the P.G.C.E. and go on to teach in further education. I did not know what the P.G.C.E. course contained but decided to follow it to prove that I could cope with post-graduate work. Deep down I did not want to go back to lifting television sets and saw the P.G.C.E. as a way out. I followed the P.G.C.E. course at Bolton College of Education (Tech.) and found the tuition to be very poor. The lecturers were uninspiring and uninformative and handouts were much dated. Teaching practice was however very useful, and like me others found this the most valuable part of the P.G.C.E. course. I did my teaching practice in a highly technically orientated college and this proved a useful baptism into the profession. In 1972 there were a number of vacancies in further education and I was lucky enough to be called for four interviews. I cancelled two, one from a school and the other one because it was some distance from my home. I had a serious disagreement with the Principal on my first interview and rejected the job offered. On my second interview I sought clarification on a point referring to race - as by now I felt confident in taking on anyone on this topic -and on the structure and authority of interviewing panels. I was however offered the post and accepted.

Having joined the profession full-time, I set about clarifying my ideas and means of communication with students. I was aware of my limitations and realised that

I must not take for granted knowledge supposedly held by the students. There is racism in the college, both from staff and students, and directed to the Black students. There is no organised teaching on issues of race except through some subjects like psychology and sociology, and it is an issue the college hierarchy seem to feel uneasy about. I have, since completion of my P.G.C.E. gained my Masters degree and am at present following a Ph.D. programme. I feel that I have not done as well as I could in terms of occupation, and that may be due to two factors. Firstly, I do not sell myself and perhaps I ought to, and secondly, I have been reluctant to apply for posts in other cities or abroad due to family ties. I have reviewed both situations. I have no evidence, practical or emotional to support the view that my race is the reason for my not obtaining a senior post or more challenging work in my field. This may be so, as I am not privy to discussions on applications that I have submitted. I am however hopeful that something will come up. Education to me has been useful, and is a central concern in my present thinking. I would not be where I am were it not for the education I received. Having said that I should add that much of what I got from education was despite its traditions, structure and personnel, which at times would have led me towards failure. I also learnt much away from the system, which I found not only complimentary but central to understanding what the system was all about.

Peter was born into a very large and rather poor family in rural Trinidad. He did not feel specially deprived, because of the prevalence of real poverty in the local community. He received a basic elementary school education, but family reserves were not sufficient to secure for him a secondary education. This was a deprivation he felt bitterly; it contributed to his life-long determination to make his own way from level to level of the post-school system.

At each juncture in his educational career, the lack of information and advice has been strikingly evident. He could so easily have been helped to make quicker progress, and to find a less burdensome route through the system. His great persistence, and his unflagging application to learning tasks have however carried him through to a level somewhat above that of most indigenous graduates. Over this long period he identifies four people where support during the different phases of learning has been crucial for him.

He has experienced problems of language and conceptualisation in higher education, especially on first entry. He finds this to be a frequent problem among Black students, calling for further analysis.

All his study in Britain, from 'O' level to post-M.Ed., has been at the adult level. During this experience he has encountered little racism, except from a psychology lecturer during his degree course.

He found racism to be rife among his teaching colleagues in further education, which surprised him.

He is convinced that racism influences the performance of Black students in education. In particular, it leads them to distrust their own abilities.

He has experienced problems of language and conceptualisation in higher education, especially on first entry. He finds this to be a frequent problem among Black students, calling for further analysis.

SIGNIFICANT THEMES

ON BEING BRITISH

'I responded like many other colonials to a call for
an effort against Hitler.... our efforts were never
mentioned in despatches, and the war films made of men
never portray Black faces and this annoys me.'
(case history 10)

This view may help to convey the motivations and
decisions that stimulated the migration and settlement of
Black people - mainly of Afro-West Indian origin, in
Britain after 1900. The case histories show that the need
for further and higher education, an economic motive and a
patriotic response are the underlying factors that
generated such a movement.

Those who came brought with them valued knowledge and
skills, which was a drain on their country of origin and a
gain to their country of adoption. This transfer of
educational capital, i.e. knowledge and skills, is one
manifestation of a world wide phenomenon observed during
the last fifty years. The 'brain drain' is not peculiar to
third world countries, as scientists and other specialists,
each of whom cost thousands of pounds to educate, emigrated
from Britain to the United States decades ago. This third

world's loss to the first world is, however, more dramatic because of the former's acute economic situation.

It is interesting to note, in this context, the experience of countries in the second world. The iron curtain across Eastern Europe is often misunderstood. It was erected largely to prevent the loss of highly trained specialists to the West, particularly, West Germany. As soon as the Berlin wall was made effective the economy of East Germany took off on a steady rise.

Being British meant more than being one of her majesty's colonials to the Black people who came mainly from the West Indies to settle in this land. It was the outcome of an economic and social link forged at a much earlier period, and generated specific psychological responses. Because of this, these people expected a warm welcome, and this was understood to be reciprocal, as manifested in the behaviour of West Indians to White Britons who visited, or settled in, the Caribbean islands; "....I found a common theme running through my visit, no matter which island I happened to be in at the time. I do not think I have ever experienced such hospitality. I do not mean the glossy smile reserved for the tourists, but the genuine 'c'mon man, you are one of the family' type of welcome."

This 'family' feeling is central to the concept of being British. It is shared by most of the respondents, though following their experience of living in Britain such a view now seems somewhat tarnished.The 'roots' of 'being British' are historical, and relate to what many writers see as a relationship between the 'metropolitan' (a colonising authority) and the satellite (the colonised). It is a relationship not uniquely British, but specifically European in its genesis. Many notable Black writers like Fanon, Rodney and Cabral have commented on this link from which the concept 'mother country' originates.

With reference to the West Indies, Lewis best illustrates this point :'....they have lost most of their African heritage, assimilating the ideas of their white rulers, and adapting themselves to European institutions. English is spoken universally (though there are remnants of French patois) and Christianity has replaced African religions'. Lewis's view is important in understanding this umbilical relationship which pays special attention to education and religion. It is not, therefore, an accident that institutions in the satellite countries resemble those of the metropolitan, and that most holders of office in such countries, be they political, judicial, medical, technical or academic, sought and received a metropolitan-based education. This process of 'metropolitanisation' is seen through Fanon's concept of the 'evelue' i.e. the creation of a separate class of Blacks from the indigeneous Black population - and Rodney's 'Black bourgeoisie'. Rodney noted that colonial education was not designed to promote pride in one's own society but to instil a sense of deference towards all that was European and capitalist. Rodney utilized an admission of Dr. Kofi Busia (Ghana) to illustrate his point : 'Over the years as I went through College and University, I felt increasingly that the education I received taught me more about Europe and less and less about my own society'.

The fact that all the writer's respondents saw education as a central mechanism for change, both on a personal level and as members of a racial group comes as no surprise. The desire to be educated as one reason for emigrating to Britain is commonplace, and again not surprising. Of the writers already mentioned Fanon (Martinique) was educated in Paris Cabral (Portuguese Guinea) was educated in Lisbon, and Rodney (Guyana) in Britain. The significance of the movement to the 'mother country' is illustrated in the thoughts of C.L.R. James, one of the most eminent of Black scholars. James states 'the origins of my work and my thoughts are to be found in Western European Literature, Western European history and Western European thought' and he adds 'we were black and the only way we could do anything along the lines we were interested in was by going abroad : that's how I grew up.' James came to England in 1932, aged thirty one. This also is conveyed by Frank Reeves in a recent article 'We had all been given the impression of a land of remarkably intelligent white people from the fact that Englishmen had written most of our school textbooks. In addition, we had been taught that England was our mother country and we tended to imagine a mother as a source of warmth and understanding.'

Walvin states 'What seems to have shocked Jamaican settlers in Britain was that the British did not even accept or even know about the particular levels or status, skill or achievement already attained by arriving

Jamaicans.   Jamaicans were, in British eyes, an
undifferentiated group of poor black immigrants.'
    The respondents on the whole displayed an unshakeable
belief in the British way of life, including the view that
education was the key to economic and social status.
Arrival and settlement in Britain, the mother country, laid
bare the basic contradiction facing Black people.   The
reality of the situation is ably sketched by Lester and
Bindman ".... the English view never regarded the mother
country as a land of open spaces and unlimited opportunity,
but rather as a place of restricted possibilities and
fairly fixed social position, with emigration the
alternative for the restless and ambitious." This finds
some support in an article by T. Allen. He states 'At the
beginning of the C.17th appalling conditions of poverty and
disease afflicted the British people, far worse than any
crisis affecting the Caribbean island at the time of large
scale emigration in the 1950's and 60's.   The people of
Britain found escape routes to improve their precarious
conditions in the colonies, overseas including the British
Caribbean. Over-population, land hunger and disease forced
them to emigrate on a far larger scale than that of
Caribbean migration in the present century.   History
repeated itself but in the reverse direction when West
Indians - themselves a product of enforced British
migration - set out to seek economic refuge by emigration
to England'.
    On the British attitude to subjected peoples, Walvin
alerts us to the treatment of the Jews; a people who,
according to him became somewhat incorrectly synonymous
with the word 'immigrant'.   As commonwealth (Black)
immigration provoked argument during the 1960's, so did
Jewish settlement between 1881 and 1905.   Walvin writes
'the turmoil in which Europe was plunged by the rise of
expansive and aggressive Fascism, particularly Nazism, was
felt initially by the political (and religious) opponents
of those regimes.' None were to be more traumatized than
German and later European Jews who bore the brunt of Nazi
violence.   'It is perfectly true that anti-semitism was a
pronounced and undeniable feature of British life among,
for example, the upper classes who sympathised overtly with
Oswald Mosley's British fascists and especially in the
fashionable coterie which clung to Nazi diplomats in
London.... there were many Britons who did not welcome

European Jews, however bestial the regime from which they had fled.'

Notwithstanding the difference in racial origin, the writer found that the common experience of racism by the Jews and Blacks often led to positive assistance between the groups. "My first job was in a factory that made clothes. While working there, I was told by one of the girls that after my interview, Mr Blake the boss (the firm was owned by Jewish people) called the workforce together, about forty of them and warned them all that if any of them passed any remark or try to humiliate me, they would be seriously dealt with. This was interesting because I worked there for six months before I knew that.' (Case History 11).

Walvin also reports on the racism towards the Irish. His work shows that when the Irish came to England in the nineteenth century as the Jamaicans in the twentieth century, they were confronted with much hostility. Many people see the Irish, of all immigrants to Britain, as the most compatible with their hosts. They are White, Christian and speak the same language. Walvin is quick to correct this view. He reports that prejudice against them has always run deep. Brian Parsons in a recent article emphasises this turbulent relationship, noting that racism in both its anti-Black and anti-Irish contexts pre-dates large scale immigration. He states 'as early as 1700, over a century before the advent of social Darwinism with its elaborate pseudo-scientific racial theories, there were already ample signs that the Irish had been allotted, in English perceptions, an inferior status that was frequently compared with the subject and colonised peoples....the Irish is viewed as a coward in his own country, a lusty stallion in England, a graceful footman in France, a good soldier in Flanders and a valuable slave in our Western plantations where they are distinguished by the ignominious epithet of white negroes.'

The Poles were grudgingly allowed to settle in Britain. They themselves perceived their situation as different in that their exile was not economic but of a specific political situation. Walvin reports that the British Government wished for their return to Poland and the public generally supported this view.

Walvin reminds us that the peoples of the Indian sub-continent fared no better than the Jews and West Indians.

They, like others of the Commonwealth, responded to the call during the war years and record 36,000 dead, a fact generally written out of history. A reaction to their presence in Britain today is reported by Amrit Wilson. The following is an extract from an experience of one of the many Asian families in her study. 'Last Saturday night they were watching television. They had just had the windows repaired from the last volley of stones. Fists started hammering on their windows. They turned the lights out and sat in fear.'

Being British and perceiving of a 'mother' that is understanding, welcoming and warm, has exacted an enormous cost on Black people. The most hurtful is the denial of full participation on grounds of colour.

These histories illustrate the views of those who experienced this 'English dilemma'. I was also surprised by the reaction of the people to me when I went to church with the family. The congregation obviously did not want me there, (Case History 11). An even more damning testimony was the following 'looking back now I think of the loyalty we had for England. We would have done anything for her. Sadly, I no longer have this feeling for her after my experiences in this country'. (Case History 14). Even those Black people born in this country hold a jaundiced view of Britain. 'I remember my mother making the most beautiful parties for me and nobody would come. I thought something was wrong with me." (Case history 11).

Black people's experience of the 'English dilemma' generated a gulf between expectation and reality, and fractured the ideology of the 'mother country', especially among second and third generation Blacks. The older generation still sometimes clings to the belief in 'British fair-play' as case histories 2, 3 and 4.

The case histories also show that Black people are eager to participate fully and constructively for Britain if given the opportunity and document the fact that as a people they are aware of the undeniable fact that racism is a feature of British life. Many acknowledge that racism persists due to a lack of historical knowledge about Black people and their contribution to Britain in times of war as in times of peace.

OUT OF SCHOOL

Racism influences the employment and training
opportunities of members of the Black community and this
fact makes for a 'push' factor into other ways of making a
living. Sport is one such alternative, acting as the
'pull' factor in its popularity amongst the community.
Paul Hoch sees this push-pull factor as intricately tied up
with western capitalism, and designed to divert the
energies of the Black community into meaningless channels.
Ernest Cashmore disagrees with this view. He however,
supports the argument which holds that sport attracts many
Black youngsters who are often frustrated by the
inaccessibility to other forms of employment. In
dismissing Hoch's view, Cashmore quotes 'my biases are
already clear: I see sport as a supremely creative
enterprise in which the competitor exerts a mastery and
control over himself and his environment.' Cashmore's data
shows this view to be unrealistic. He underscores the
alienating aspects of sport as a mode of existence to both
participants and their families. On the other hand, Hoch's
view of sport as an instrument of total capitalist
domination may be some distance from the truth, as Black
people cannot be seen as unresponsive to the socioeconomic
influences; many are willing participants whilst others

reject it as a central influence on their lives.

The truth may lie somewhere between Hoch's and Cashmore's views. While sport may be fulfilling for the participants, we cannot totally deny the view that sport mirrors certain aspects of the social system. It fosters the stereotype that the Black person is a good athlete and little else.

Paul Hoch states 'by ignoring the socioeconomic environment that shapes sporting activities we are ignoring any possibility of understanding the place of sports in our society and the way in which involvement in sport affects the lives of people'. If we consider Hoch's argument we may agree that sport forms part of that larger aspect of the socialisation process that encourages the Black person to accept that his or her transition into sport is a natural one, as against participation in the more formal and traditional occupational roles especially at the professional and senior professional level. To this extent then Hoch would see sport as influencing the 'fit', 'cog-like roles' between Black people and the economic system of this country.

What this study did indicate was that many Blacks were encouraged by their teachers to favour sporting activities, often at the expense of formal studies. This is supported by many of the study's respondents who had any inclination to sport (see case histories 1, 7, 16, 26, 27). It was not unusual for the teachers to foster an interest in sport in order to obtain honours for the school and in turn the student's life becomes dominated by the sport.

Cashmore in his studies reports the case of Mickey Morris, whose testimony bears this out. Cashmore noted that conflict between Mickey and the teachers came when he refused to play in a school football match which clashed with a geography lesson. Mickey was castigated by the teacher and told he was letting the school down. This pressure was common among many of Cashmore's respondents: 'for many black kids sport is central, not because the other areas are seen as worse risks but because they are seen as less accessible. They believe that there are only limited numbers of entrances to the upper reaches of the employment world.... the props for such beliefs come from within the black community; black children tell each other stories about how difficult it is to get a decent job if you are black'. Unfortunately many of those cajoled into sports realised later on what they were not good enough to make a living from sport and end up the loser, in that the school did not prepare them for any alternative path. (see case history 7.)

This decision in the early years of schooling does affect many students regardless of race, but society is less well disposed towards the Black person in these circumstances. Paul Hoch states 'no doubt the exploitation of the white athlete is almost equally ruthless. He too gets his share of junk courses. Gives his all to the team, while the college collects the profit. He, too, a large part of the time, never graduates. But he also has a lot of job opportunities his black team-mates do not. He has not been so thoroughly coaxed into believing that sport is his best chance to make it in life'.

Garth Crooks' experience further substantiates this point. He states 'black kids feel that they have a much better chance of achieving something in sport than they have in other areas of society....black kids in Britain tend to lose a little bit of ground in school. They lose interest and then fall behind and this disadvantages them. But in sport they see the chance of being number one, and, as a result, they give it their complete and total interest'.

Cashmore firmly believes that free choice dominates entry. Having arrived in sport, Cashmore sees failure as a reflection of a lack of family commitment to their offspring's cause. He states 'the passive role of the black family in their children's sport jars with the discordance of a cracked bell when compared to the part played by the white family, usually a source of encouragement from which affirmative strengthening and when necessary consoling influences come'.

The parents' reason for this lack of involvement is only pursued by Cashmore to the extent that he sees the parents as having no time available nor money to squander on what they consider to be pointless pursuits. The writer's brief foray into this area confirms the view that many Black parents see sport as a waste of time, not a 'proper job', a response which is the result of a socialising process which recognises the lack of educational status and uncertain economic advantage in sport. Mr Bangbala's (case history 3) response to his son's (case history 4) wish to pursue a career in football is evidence of this. 'I matriculated in July 1948, wanting to be a professional footballer as I was a good sportsman, but my father would not hear of it. Nothing other than going to learn a trade'. This reaction was in concert with that of other parents in this study, and it is a view which is emphasised in an article by Horace Lashley concerning the low priority PE has in schools. Lashley notes 'the Black community has not recognised prowess on the sports field as genuine educational success: indeed, too much involvement and over-representation in sports may be keeping black youngsters from the classroom'. The parents, like Lashley, feel that sport only provides a limited outlet for secure employment, if at all. They see the central purpose of schooling to be steady and secure employment afterwards.

The parents believe that employment in the more traditional fields like education, medicine and the law are less likely to harbour such racism. The young Black participant, on the other hand, sees sport as a leveller, a situation where only performance on the field of play counts. This view is soon tarnished by the reality that confronts the Black sportsperson, as substantiated in this study's case histories 1, 7, 13 and 26; and by Cashmore. He states 'whatever his illusions before changing his priority to sport, the black youth finds that his chosen area is not so different from the rest of society'.

Racism as part of their experience in sport features high on the list of responses of all Cashmore's study participants, and some, like Maurice Hope, saw sport as a way to vent his frustration and release aggression. Many had to contend with such attitudes inside the game, from their colleagues and sometimes management (see case history 7). They also had to cope with it from certain sections of the public within the stadia (see case history 13). The activities on the terraces is seen by many as a mirror reflecting the increase in racism as documented in Glen Cooksley's article, in which he includes a piece from Eric Moonman's study, 'Football and the Fascists'. The piece notes that few in the game believe that the football clubs are doing enough to challenge right-wing racist recruitment among its supporters.

MUSIC

Music is another alternative for the frustrated ambitions of the Black school leaver, and the influences motivating the youths toward particular music type is not without racist implications. Like sport it transmits a negative stereotype for Black youth, i.e. the 'natural' ability that relates to their sporting prowess is also linked to their sense of natural rhythm, as the following extract from a Nursery Nursing text on care of Black children in nurseries. 'West Indian children can be lively, boisterous and responsive. Their feeling for music and rhythm often makes it physically impossible for them to remain still when music is being played'.

There is an absence of published material on the transition from school to an involvement in the production and presentation of Black cultural music, e.g. Reggae etc. by Black school leavers, a production which entails constructing sound systems, and the marketing of the distinctive sounds produced, i.e. D.J.ing (disc-jockeying) for varied functions. Another feature of this transition is the setting up of the more formal framework allowing for the emergence of such Black pop groups as Aswad, Matumbi and Misty. While no documentation was to hand on the world of sound systems at the time of writing, Colin Macdonald does provide us with a brief look into the type of workshops from which the more formal type of Black pop group emerges. He notes that his music workshop was set up in response to requests from local Black youths to try out playing music together, and confirms the view held by one of this study's respondents who states 'I was really interested in music at school but was not encouraged.... the music teacher was only interested in Beethoven and stuff like that'. (Case history 8).

Macdonald found that while many teachers have made valuable inroads into the use of rock and reggae, the traditional view of music still persists. In the workshop, he claims, the youths are able to attempt a wide mix of music styles which reflect the attitudes and interests of the community. To Macdonald this is a "celebratory" form expressing a sense of shared experience both social and political that is integrated with daily life rather than being something that is reserved for the concert hall.

Barry Troyna's article suggests to us that this link with 'cultural' music is fostered by the youths while still at school. It enables them to cope with the frustrations of schooling. 'They channelled their energies to ethnic sources for support'. Troyna found that in doing so they ensured further failure in school. This adherence to an ethnic culture which allows for a form of artistic expression is also seen as the youths' response to their perception of the economic crisis; as Ken Pryce noted 'for hustlers and teenyboppers the music business is a way of earning a living'. Pryce feels that the music business offers the Black youth the possibility of escape from obscurity and inferiority, while at the same time allowing for the opportunity to imbibe a sense of ideological and cultural solidarity into their life style.

This solidarity is essential for the disaffected in a society that devalues Black people, and the response of 'gut' music is one way of expressing their feelings and distancing their oppressor. Paul Gilroy notes that the speech pattern of Reggae is a mechanism for achieving this goal. He states 'such language is able to convey commitment in a selective or intermittent manner, and its racially exclusive mode invites speakers to appropriate ideas which appeal to them without being pigeon-holed by the oppressor'.

What is often overlooked and remains largely unrecognised is the intellectual sophistication involved in the presentation of such music. Through the sound system the D.J. has to rely on oral skill which has a long pedigree, and is termed toasting(to speak over recorded music, improvising on the lyrics and creating a new version). Quick-wittedness and verbal skills are required to accomplish this task. Another form of presentation is Dub lyricism (to speak lines of poetry overdubbed with instrumental backing). Paul Gilroy notes that the Dub process is the dominant form of Reggae, and is an intrinsic element of the social relations in which all Reggae reveals its power, a power which symbolises the political struggle that the Black community is involved in.

The writer's observation suggests that this form of community involvement is quite large, though the school's response to it in curricula terms is negligible; in that it is only seriously addressed in a few schools, among them Tulse Hill School (case history 21), where Caroline Davis organises such work. The traditional view of music in the curriculum persists and seemingly fails to stimulate but a few Black youths. The writer was fortunate in being introduced to one of the few Black youths involved in this form of music. His interesting story appears in case history 9.

Perhaps an education system that sees Black youths as working class, spontaneous and excitable, by its very nature will fail to attract, or be loath to welcome, Black youths to its more European traditional approach to music. It is no wonder that Tommy (case history 9) enquires 'it interests me to know why there are not many Black people in classical music, except in the States'.

THE POLICE

The literature on the relationship between Black people and the police is extensive, and it is not the intention here to provide a comprehensive review. The purpose is to tune in the respondents' experience to some of it. Sadly, many of the writers, e.g. Paul Gilroy, 1982, support the experience of respondents. It is one of police harrassment, racial abuse and maltreatment. Mr Marke (case history 2) tells us of such experiences at the turn of the century, especially his witness of the Liverpool disturbances of 1919. It is a pattern of behaviour which continues to the present day (see case histories 16, 26, 27, 28 and note the writer's altercation with the police in case history 28).

The attitude and actions of the police, and the educational experience, are central issues in 'consciousness of race' among this community. The 'hunger' of Sivanandan's quote is not an expression of Britain in the 1930s, but a Britain in the eighties wishing to be free of racial repression. It is a hunger expressed by Leroy Cooper, a Black resident of Toxteth, Liverpool, 'I won't accept the lie-down-and-take-it attitude that my parents accepted. In 1985 the youth is becoming politically aware especially since 1981'.

Not so long ago Professor Stuart Hall in a visionary lecture to the Cobden Trust provided us with a frame of reference on the policing of Black people. Professor Hall commented on the use of police power to contain, constrain and to criminalise parts of the Black population. He states 'not all the stories and rumours are, of course, true. Not all of them traceable to racism within the local police force. But when all reasonable allowances have been made, this series of episodes leaves us with no other conclusion than that the police have undertaken -whether willingly or not - to constrain, by means which would not long stand up to inspection within the rule of law, an alienated Black population: and thereby, to police the social crisis of the cities.'

The repression emphasised by Professor Hall is known to extend beyond the police, to the courts. An enquiry shows that young Black offenders make a disproportionately high number of court appearances compared with their White counterparts. They are also more likely to be jailed or receive some other custodial sentence than White young people of the same age group. Even ten years ago a memorandum from the National Council of Civil Liberties recorded their considered opinion that the worsening situation between the police and the Black community is very serious. The Council accepted the view that once the local community has lost confidence in the police, it will act accordingly and will interpret all police action as hostile. This view is also emphasised in the Scarman Report.

The lack of trust also manifests itself in the general unwillingness of members of the Black community to accept a career in the police force. The one respondent (see case history 1) in this study whose career ambitions extended to the police service experienced a degree of racism which led to her resignation. Her experience is supported by the recent disclosure of racism within the Metropolitan Police Training School. Mr. Fernandes, a civilian lecturer at the school, leaked to the press some racist essays written by his students -police cadets. Mr Fernandes was sacked for the disclosure and later had difficulty in gaining union support.

Such attitudes as held by the police were taken up by Professor Moore, who cited a Manchester Community Relations report which showed that policemen were inclined to believe that immigrants are more criminal than the population at large. On the other hand publications by Professor Michael Banton in 1964 and 1975 show that the public lack trust in negative reports on the police. It is a view that gained support from Chief Constable James Anderton when he hit back at criticism of the police after five teenage boys were beaten up by officers in Islington, London. The police chief said that the earnest intention of the police service was to get rid of unworthy members. (The officers concerned were later convicted and sentenced.) Professor Robert Moore challenges this public view. Moore states 'the idea that our policemen are wonderful, but there are a few "bad apples" in the barrel will hold no water.... the police are actually in conflict with the black community. The policeman sees himself in the front line of defence against the blacks'. A result of this is that despite police attempts to heighten their presence in schools and make for better community relations, some members of the community and their teachers have refused to co-operate with them.

This conflict with the forces of law and order is also manifest in the attitude of many organisations within the community, from the Pan-Africanists of the 1940s through the Black Power Movements of the late sixties, the Luther King crusade, Rastafarianism and the Caribbean Teachers Association of the present time. (All the organisations are firmly rooted in Britain). A common feature of such groups is that they tend to have links with religious organisations. The correlation between the forces of order, the church and education is not a new one. To Black people this link has a long history and is of special relevance to their members resident in Britain. It is interesting to note that many of the respondents in this study talked of the influence of religious organisations on their education. Some saw religion as a force for change (see case histories 22 and 23), others saw it as an oppressive and negative force (see case histories 1 and 11), while to some it was a mechanism, for escaping from the realities of life in Babylon (see case histories 16 and 19).

RELIGION

In the light of the uprisings in Britain's inner cities, high unemployment and deprivation among Black people, both Black and White stress the need for 'the church' to consider its involvement and its approach to the problems faced by the Black community in Britain. To many the Biblical language and its message seem far removed from their situation, providing a site for psychological release, and not a constructive force for change. There is no doubt, however, that for some religion could provide for a radical change. This point is clearly stated in Mr Carter's (case history 22) comparison of the British and American situation 'we have not developed a Black psyche as have our American brothers and sisters. We have not because our churches have not yet consolidated to educate the community'.

While acknowledging the growing need for change in the community, some of the respondents note that the church has yet to endorse it. The issue is universal, and poignantly expressed in the comments of Che Guevara 'when the Christians have the courage to commit themselves completely to the revolution.... the revolution will be invincible'.

This view that religion should be party to the secular

activities of the community is not only that of radical
political figures outside the church, but also of some
churchmen.   Rev. James H. Cone, a Black American writer,
minister of the church and Professor of Theology, finds
that many contemporary theologians are silent about the
disadvantaged condition of Black people.   To him, such
theologians see no relationship between Black oppression
and the Christian gospel;   consequently there has been no
sharp confrontation with White racism.

While Cone's view still holds true, in some parts of
the world religious movements are putting up a vigorous
challenge.   It is worth noting that the ecumenical church
view in Britain is addressing itself to this issue.   The
theology of liberation relates well to the peoples of
Africa, especially Southern Africa, and to South America,
but sits uneasily with religious activities in Britain.
The reason for this, as Ken Pryce supports, is that ours is
a religion of accommodation, not confrontation.   Pryce
notes that religion to the Black person assists in his or
her interpretation of the world and stimulates the
development of strategies for survival.   It is clear, he
states, that the religion of 'saints' is a religion of the
oppressed and that in their sermons and style of worship,
saints are interpreting Christianity in order to satisfy
their own needs as working class Blacks in a White racist
society.   It is, he states, a response which helps them to
cope with their sense of alienation and powerlessness.

This is a response far removed from the
liberationists' views and the recent pronouncements of some
churches in Britain.   The Right Reverend David Jenkins,
Bishop of Durham, writing on the subject feels that while
British Liberation theology will take some of the diagnoses
of Marxism very seriously, it will not in any way be
dominated by Marxism.   'We must work out our own liberation
theology related to our needs'.   Bishop Jenkins sees one
aspect of this theology as developing economic and other
resources to combat attitudes, events and 'statistics'
which suggest that the substantial minority of our fellows
are second and third class citizens, or not citizens at
all.

Ten years ago the World Council of Churches adopted
the line taken by Bishop Jenkins.   On this occasion the
Council felt that as Christians all forms of violence must
be rejected and the principle of direct non-violent action

seen as the way to bring an end to recalcitrant racist structures. The Council, however, saw itself standing firmly on the side of the oppressed, even though violence may at times be present. 'It is the hope that such desperate acts on the part of the oppressed will no longer be necessary'.

Such a view is parallel to Adventists' thinking. It is a religion that draws heavily from the Black community. They are interested in change through evangelism and education. The anti-political ethos stems not simply from pre-millenarists' rejection of the 'world' but from the highly specific eschatology which imputes to the state a crucial role in the series of events which to Adventists precede the second coming of Christ.

Responding to this is the experience of Mr. Woodford, who leads an all-Black Adventist school in North London, (case history 24). Mr Woodford finds that many members of the Black community, Adventists and non-Adventists, confronted with the problems forced on them by society - especially in their relations with their children - tend to see an Adventist education as a major means of combating the damaging influences of this secular society.

Robin Theobold points out that a commitment to Adventism and its way of life provides the additional advantage of increased educational and professional status. He states 'it is certain that the West Indian sector of British Adventism contains a substantially higher proportion of individuals in middle class occupations than in the West Indian population at large'. Mr Woodford goes further in making the link between Adventism and wider political action. He states 'given the fact that we have a school that works, access to the media because of the special nature of the school, it is possible to make political statements. This will throw me in the political arena to operate for the benefit of Black people from a priveleged base. I resist this because to get this place to function within the church needs total commitment'.

Many members of the Black community look to the church for some positive influence to change the situation they find themselves in. They want the church to address the social, political and educational issues that surround their lives. It is naive to suggest, as Roy Kerridge does, that the great issue among West Indians in England is 'not police persecution or any political cause, but the division

between the saved and the unsaved'. For a large percentage
of Black people in Britain the education of their children
and increased political awareness is at the forefront of
their minds. Many turn to religion in the hope that the
church will make for some positive change in their
lifestyle. Recent events suggest that they will not be
altogether disappointed.

FAMILY PATTERNS

'Received Wisdom' about the culture and structure of the Black (Afro West Indian) family continues to suggest that family characteristics are the cause of the many problems experienced by Black people in Britain. This claim is especially virulent regarding 'Blacks' reported negative performance in the education system. For this reason it is useful to examine such a view briefly in light of the respondent's comments.

Ray Honeyford, recent headmaster of a Bradford school, is on record as supporting this widely held view. He states 'the roots of black educational failure are in reality, located in the West-Indian family structure and values'. It is a claim also supported by Ernest Cashmore in recent writings. Cashmore, however, qualifies the thrust of his remarks on this issue by stating that he empathizes with the Black family and the situation they find themselves in, having to cope with the pressures militating against them. However, he goes on to suggest that disorganised family backgrounds and parents unsympathetic to the educational needs of their children are responsible for Black childrens' failure in the education system.

It is also not uncommon for official bodies to link such family patterns to academic underachievement. When this occurs authoritative validation is given for such claims, and it becomes the point of focus, omitting the more positive influences of the Black family and their involvement with their members education. The Swann Report can be placed in this category. It states that the influence of the wider social structure is to blame for Black underachievement but it endorses the view that West Indian children's low attainment is related to their family pattern. An article on Swann in the Guardian states 'the social and economic circumstances of the children's families have a lot to do with their performance in school'. The article goes on to suggest that family values are influential in this process. The fact that the Black family is still seen as a major contributor to their members' academic failure, while external influences are underplayed, remains a cause for concern, and is very relevant today. The reader may well enquire as to what exactly is this Black family pattern. How did it originate?

Ken Pryce in his research on West Indian life styles in Bristol, provides us with an answer. He states 'all researchers into the problem have drawn attention to the proliferation of "common law" or "non-legal" unions among lower class folk, and social reformers have been most worried about them. Among the upper and middle classes, the monogamous nuclear family and Christian marriages are the ideal which generally speaking, they adhere to. Further down the scale, however, the situation changes. Family life is more unstable. In the early stages of adult life instead of a man and a woman getting married and setting up their own separate household for procreation and domestic purposes, the partners live apart with their separate kin and the man visits his mate,.... if the common union endures long enough to take the form of "faithful concubinage", the partners will marry each other. These practices stem directly from the institution of slavery, which was responsible for the total destruction of conventional family life among slaves'.

The attractiveness of this anthropological view posited as a reason for Black underachievement persists. Eurocentricism does not allow its writers to pursue an objective analysis. Such an analysis, if put forward, will no doubt raise many other points worth considering, such as following: firstly, it is likely that such a family pattern has undergone and is undergoing change, due to generational influences, e.g. some respondents' views in this study tell us that it is unlikely that the majority of children of later generations hold similar values to their parents. Secondly, one should take into account the rising popularity of co-habitation among the indigenous White population to see to what extent family instability as an influence on educational achievement has occurred. Thirdly, one needs to question and compare the stability of European Christian marriages with the West Indian pattern. One notes the ever increasing British divorce and separation rates suggesting that three in five men and one in two women will experience divorce.

The view that social pathology afflicting British people can be traced to the instability of the family structure and its values is challenged by Sally Tomlinson. She states 'these studies may have contributed to a continued stereotyping of West-Indian families as somehow more disorganised and less responsible than other parents. It is relatively commonplace to hear West Indian family life compared unfavourably to Asian family life in Britain, on the basis of little or no evidence'.

Similar criticism comes from J. Hodges et al in their analysis of hierarchical control in the family. It is also interesting to note the ambivalence in research on the Black family. On the one hand the family's capacity to cope with social pressures has impressed, yet this same family pattern is perceived as an obstacle to progress, an obstacle explained through the concept 'cultural lag' as a product of resettlement. F. Znaniecki's observations of Polish families, though dated, illustrates this point. He looked at families before and after immigration using the Gemeinschaft (rural) Gesellschaft (urban) contrast. He noted that the force of community - a rural manifestation - that held them together was threatened by the disintegrative power of urbanisation. This force was to have less effect on the second generation and beyond. Though aspects of their culture survived, much of the old familiar pattern gave way to models of their adopted country. A similar process may have influenced the settlement of Black families in Britain, who had to cope with, and at times resist, disintegrative influences on

their lives. It is this struggle to maintain values and
ethnic identity that is seen as an obstacle and is a point
of disagreement, perhaps because of a misunderstanding.
     Anne Phizaklea's study of Jamaican women in Harlesden
well illustrates this point. Phizaklea observed that the
position of West Indian working mothers is misunderstood.
She points out that West Indian women have a long history
of migration in search of work. 'The fact that a woman can
be motivated to migrate in order to achieve her own social
and economic goal is never given credence'. This work
notes that such misunderstandings and the external
influences which are likely to follow in an attempt to
Europeanise the Black family can at best be considered
'cultural imperialism' and at worst crude racism. Such
misunderstandings often lead to intervention by state
agents of social control. Institutions, or members of such
institutions, seek to enforce conformity to the norms and
values of this society in education; with miscegenous
relationships; and on rights of settlement.
     Respondents' information shows that decisions on
schooling were often carried through without parental
consent and with no preliminary contact with the family.
Case History 19 illustrates this point. 'When I heard I
was going to "special school" I was very sad because I knew
I was going to leave my friends'. In this case the
student's parents were informed after the decision was
made, and while this may be seen as not unusual,
investigations proved otherwise.
     Sally Tomlinson commenting on this point brings to our
attention the guidelines set by Bradford City Council,
which holds that it is important that minority group
parents should, as should all parents, be made familiar
with the nature of schooling their children are receiving.
Tomlinson notes that such guidelines setting out the rights
of parents are laid down by the 1944 and 1980 Education
Acts. While the information gathered from respondents in
this work does not show an in-depth knowledge of the 1944
nor the 1980 Education Acts, it does show parental concern
and willingness to be involved with their childrens'
education, as is evidenced in the following statement 'my
mother always fought my school battles while my father more
or less advised us on the work situation, trade unions and
that'. (Case History 5).
     As indicated, external influences on the family life

of Black people were not uncommon, and respondents'
accounts show that such influences often led to
intervention where interracial relationships occurred.
This issue was a central concern of Parliament during the
1950's and touched the lives of many Black families in
Britain.   Paul Foot noted that the then Commonwealth
Secretary, Patrick Gordon Walker, took a reactionary line
on the Seretse Khama affair.   'Almost his first job as
Commonwealth Secretary in 1950 was to inform the Commons
that Seretse Khama, Chief of the Bamangwto tribe in
Bechuanaland was to be banned from returning to this
country because he had married a white woman'.   Many
respondents' accounts suggest that the views expressed by
Mr. Patrick Gordon Walker had the sympathy of White
Britons.   An excerpt from case history 14 illustrates the
point 'There was also a lot of aggravation about in the
social life of Black people then.   Many Black men married
White woman as there were few Black women about.   This
caused a lot of strife amongst White men and influenced the
Government to encourage Black men to bring their wives and
girlfriends over to England'.

Where interracial unions existed amongst the early
settlers from the turn of the century, the White mother
would often negotiate on the family's behalf, often
preventing outside intervention.   Case history 11 is
indicative of this experience.   'In those days most Black
men who had White wives used to ask their wives to
negotiate with housing, education and medical authorities'.
The writer's respondents, especially those of the younger
generation hint that such practices have diminished
greatly.   This view is one which challenges that of Anne
Wilson in her account of interracial marriages.   She
supports the view of the White wife as 'the negotiator',
but also points out that this White partner felt trapped
between both races and cultures, juggling with two
different, often incompatible, roles, and compelled by the
attitude of others to experience acutely the feeling of not
being fully accepted in either racial group.

This enquiry while not focusing on this area, found
respondents' views in conflict with those of Anne Wilson.
Identity patterns seem to have altered with many more of
the Black partners in such unions being born in Britain.

Another aspect of Black family life touched on is that of the Black child born in England of a miscegenous, cohabiting relationship.   A single and dramatic example presented itself and deserves to be examined separately. It will be sufficient to note here the seriousness attached to this issue, the problems encountered by the child, the foster parents, peers and professionals concerned.

It must also be firmly stated that Black families have a long history of informal family and community care, a fact rarely perceived by professional workers.   The Black child in the situation outlined above, becomes a case for community concern.   The damaging effect of urbanization on this community response, as earlier stated, is not now as acute as in the past, as is manifest in the many recent Black groups set up to deal with the fostering of Black children.

From his repondents' experience, the writer holds that no significant aspect of the Black community can be grasped without some positive understanding of the Black family.   A move away from the negative stereotypes of its patterns is to be encouraged and we need to note the impressive progress made by such families in situations of crisis and anxiety.   The long history of the Black family in dealing with such situations makes it one of the most effective instruments in the struggle for a better life for Black people in this country.   Maureen Stone in 'The Education of the Black Child' states 'it may also be useful for social scientists, as well as identifying what they take to be the pathology of the black family and lifestyle, to devote some time to investigating the capacity for survival and cohesion amongst minority group families in the face of the oppressive - and destructive forces which characterise British and American societies in their dealings with people of African descent.' The Black family, as our data shows, places a high value on education as the key to status and a better living standard.

SOME FINDINGS

The term findings is somewhat presumptive. While this work claims that it has generated new evidence on race and adult education, a contribution to the debate is what is hoped for. The status of so-called findings remains problematic in all research.

The information gathered reveals that much of what is experienced in adult education is a result of previous encounters at school. It also tells us that there exists a predicament amongst a large minority of British citizens, and little is being done to change the situation they find themselves in. This may be because not enough is known of how they feel about major issues in their lives, and more particularly, because of the institutional racism that is so much a part of British society. The information that emerges from the data collected is often voiced by many, sometimes by few, but as already noted, the experience of Black people wherever they may live in this country is not often dissimilar.

With due regard to the above cautionary observations, the study enables the following general statements to be proposed.

1. SCHOOLING DID NOT MAKE FOR ANY SIGNIFICANT CHANGE IN THE LIVES OF MANY OF THE RESPONDENTS AND THEIR FAMILIES. This may be because the education system fails to relate its provision to what is happening in the lives of this community.

a. The school failed to inform Black children and their families of course and examination options;

b. the school failed to give guidance on requirements for local employment;

c. the school failed to inform them on the opportunities for post-school education;

d. the school failed to facilitate Black youngsters' entry into their own world of music;

e. notwithstanding all the above, Black parents generally continue to hold positive hopes and expectations of education for their children.

2. THE LACK OF CAREER GUIDANCE IN SCHOOL AND ADULT EDUCATION NEGATIVELY INFLUENCED THE LIVES OF MANY RESPONDENTS IN THE STUDY. Some of those who went on to further or higher education made course and option choices which on hindsight they felt were unwise. While teachers were seen as partly responsible for this neglect, many respondents harbour fond memories of a teacher who empathised with their situation. The respondent tended to perform well in this teacher's subject.

a. in some instances, the absence of career guidance also led to a drift away from post-school education and often from gainful employment.

3. ADULT EDUCATION PROGRAMMES WERE FOUND TO BE USEFUL TO SOME MEMBERS OF THE COMMUNITY AND INSTRUMENTAL FOR IMPROVED ECONOMIC STATUS. This confirms the view that traditionally Black people have travelled far and wide in search of education and betterment of life-style.   While adult education did provide some attempt to redress the disadvantages that occurred at school:

a.   it failed to provide programmes on managing the day-to-day issues faced by many members of the community, such as civil rights regarding the police, state benefits, consumer protection etc.

b.   most respondents felt that some teachers ' attitudes were consciously or unconsciously racist, and on occasions open discrimination was reported;

c.   a few respondents with experience of teacher education reported that racist attitudes were manifest in that system;

d.   on the basis of the experience of one respondent, it would seem plausible to accept the assertion of racism in police training.   This echoes Mr. Fernandes' experience, as reported in the body of this work;

e.   adult education, until very recently, (the Open College-Access provision) did not promote programmes to attract Blacks and to facilitate their learning and progress, especially in courses leading to professional careers. Most respondents knew little of what was on offer in further and higher education.

4.   THE CASE HISTORIES INDICATE THAT IN TIMES OF ECONOMIC PROSPERITY AND IN TIMES OF WAR, AN ETHNIC PRESENCE IS ENCOURAGED.   IN TIMES OF ECONOMIC RESTRAINT AND PEACE THEIR PRESENCE IS UNWELCOME.

a.   the evidence suggests that at all times mainly low level skills programmes are on offer for members of the Black community.

5.   YOUNG BLACKS ARE INCREASINLY BECOMING MARGINALISED AND POLITICISED.
The increased alienation that is a part of this process

encourages politicisation. The older generation notes that the absence of role models and the disappearance of an accepted faith in British 'fair play' is significant for this process.

a. the alternative activities of sport, music and hustling await this section of the community;

b. the selective emphasis on sport for Blacks is in itself racist and negative.

6. RACISM HINDERS UPWARD MOBILITY IN WORK.

a. jobs secured tend not to match held qualifications, despite laws enacted to prevent this trend;

b. serious discrimination in job training and apprenticeship continues, despite government training initiatives.

7. CONSCIOUSNESS OF SELF, RACE AND COMMUNITY IS INCREASING.

a. respondents see their problems in education and employment as discriminatory, and generated by racism; whereas sociologists, Marxists and other radicals see this and racism itself as reflecting a working class situation;

b. it would seem that the 'naming' phenomena where most Blacks prefer to be described as 'Black' (not 'coloured') has provided for a positive self-consciousness among the community. This is seen by some as a mechanism of political resistance to racism. Observations show that in education it has shaped some tutors' response to Black people.

8. BLACK WOMEN EXPERIENCE THE 'DOUBLE EDGE' OF OPPRESSION AND THIS IS NOWHERE MORE SIGNIFICANT THAN IN ADULT EDUCATION.

a. Black women and girls are resentful that as such they
    are not encouraged to be ambitious;

b. the evidence suggests that the experience of Black
    girls and women parallels that of many young Black
    men with all the added problems experienced by White
    girls, vis-a-vis boys and men;

c. despite their situation, most women and girls in the
    study seem only too ready to confront what they
    interpret as discrimination towards them or their
    families.

9. **THE PRESENCE OF A BLACK PERSON IN A POSITION OF POWER,
    ALBEIT LIMITED, TENDS TO ALTER THE DYNAMICS OF THE
    SITUATION.**

a. all the respondents who claim professional or semi-
    professional status suggest that their presence,
    either in their occupational capacity or on voluntary
    committees creates a more positive influence for the
    formation of anti-racist policies.

10. **WHILE WANTING ACCEPTANCE AND THE OPPORTUNITY TO
    PARTICIPATE FULLY IN THIS SOCIETY, BLACK PEOPLE WISH
    TO MAINTAIN THEIR OWN CULTURE AND TO PROMOTE THEIR
    HISTORY, AS DO JEWS AND OTHER ETHNIC GROUPS.**

a. the evidence suggests that the failure to achieve this
    lies, not so much with them, but with the education
    system which labels their culture as deprived,
    rejecting a way of life that is adequate and
    meaningful, but different;

b. the maintenance of their culture is seen by some
    respondents as one way of preventing the damaging
    effects of racism on personality;

c. religion as part of this culture is becoming more
    recognised by some as a positive force for political
    action and radical change;

d.   because the culture is labelled as inferior, some
      respondents feel reluctant to be part of it. This was
      observed more specifically among those of miscegenous
      unions.

The findings challenge the liberal assumption that
education makes for meaningful change in societies where
racism is present. The respondents' views indicate that
racism lies, for the present, beyond the influence of
cognitive development. While this is supported by the
evidence here presented, the data alerts us to the fact
that the situation is not stagnant.

While educational policy remains oppressive, a hidden
curriculum of anti-racism emerges as a result of pressure
from the disinherited. The force of such a movement re-
directs teaching techniques and learning attitudes, as can
be seen in the number of courses that are now presented,
conscious of the presence of the Black community. Most
respondents are conscious of a growing racism and feel that
the political and economic climate at present encourages
it. Further, some respondents are puzzled by the inability
of whites, especially working class whites, to recognise
racism and its roots.

Black respondents who occupy white collar jobs claim to
influence the decision-making process by their very
presence. This challenges the notion of 'tokenism', i.e.
that of the ineffective single Black person amongst a White
staff, an appointment made to appease those who call for
change in relations between races. This observation has
important implications for contemporary society and its
institutions.

The study may claim to have generated a number of points
that should interest the recipients of education, tutors,
the local authority, the D.E.S., and others interested in
education. It is clear that a feeling exists among Black
people disposing them to raise their level of participation
and their contribution to the education system, as it is
too important a factor in their lives to be left to
educators and administrators at present responsible for it.

The clear-cut views of many respondents were that racism

lies beyond the influence of cognitive development. This finding must be accompanied by a statement of equal weight, that this lack of penetration derives mainly from teachers' attitudes, their pedagogical instruments (e.g. books, video material, etc.) and from the media in general. Such conclusions lead us to offer the following suggestions towards access and participation in education by adult members of the Black community.

1.   That a greater awareness of the political, economic and racial situations in which Black people find themselves be promoted.

2.   That bureaucratic and financial constraints (e.g. selection systems and grant aid) placed on programmes aimed at such groups be eased.

3.   That the providers of education become more accountable to the Black people they provide for (by, for instance, the promotion of consultative and feedback systems).

4.   That the scarcity of programmes for staff development on issues of race be remedied.

5.   That the role of the YTS be further explored in relation to participation by Black young people.

6.   That a regeneration of the careers service be undertaken to take account of the needs of the Black community and Black students in particular.

7.   That the Open College concept should foster more skills courses, as not all of those returning to learn wish to go on to academic education.

8.   That educational authorities should implement strategies to eradicate institutional racism, e.g. by the use of monitoring systems.

9.   That governing bodies of educational institutions include among their representatives more Black people.

10. That more Black teaching and counselling staff be trained and appointed.

11. That the media industry be more responsible in its role as providers of information and education on issues involving Black people (e.g. by the inclusion of more Black staff members at all levels of the industry).

A NOTE ON METHOD

This is not a method-and-theory exercise. It is not organised around an hypothesis which calls for sampling and measurement. It is heuristic in that it seeks to locate important general issues through the logic of discovery in the respondents' testimonies. Many of the studies of Black people in Britain write of the Black person as an object detached from his or her own situation, often because of a positivist theoretical approach, whereas this enquiry has been concerned with the predicament of the Black community and the role that education has played in this situation.

The study aims to discover how Black people think and feel as people, what they worry about and what they anticipate. The 'web' procedure - contacting respondents across a social network - encouraged a cross-sectional take-up from a community which, though widely dispersed geographically, is almost parochial in its maintenance of fellowship. The writer's observation indicates that the constraints on Black people in this country are not fundamentally different, wherever they may live.

The open-ended unstructured interview method drew attention to other areas of concern and issues of apparent significance, but the research rests to a large extent on its historical and descriptive reportage.

The writer's research supervisor has stated 'head-counting surveys must not be allowed to become the major form of research activity in adult education and must always be seen as peripheral, as concerned with the outcome of processes rather than with the processes themselves. They should be used to support or to highlight particular aspects of investigation but should not be used in isolation'. Further support for a non-positivist research procedure in this field of human engagement comes from Professor Clyde Mitchell, of Nuffield College, Oxford. He argues strongly for an interpretative method in social science research, on epistemological grounds. He sees the arguments against it as based on a misconception of the basics from which a research may justifiably extrapolate from an individual's experience to the social processes as a whole. Professor Mitchell's stance is regarded as a very important argument in favour of the idiographic approach, highlighting as it does the importance of the individual instance. His argument provides a theoretical underpinning for the biographical method.

The research programme is therefore identified with an interpretative approach as against a positivist one. The question of which of the many procedures to apply followed. The respondents' experience, however, begged a 'life histories' approach. This considers the constant adjustment of internal relations, the processes of assimilating, making connections, making decisions, self-integration to the external relations within the family, education, work and the changing social context. The personal story focuses on individual perceptions, understandings, reactions and intentions. This contrasts with procedures that propose to extract the individual's involvement in an educational programme, and to test his response to it without considering how that response might be shaped by his life experience.

The use of the historical method lent itself to an informal in-depth interview process. A check list, not a questionnaire, was used. As can be seen, the points on the list were posed in everyday language in an open form to encourage the respondents to tell his or her own story.

Having decided on how to go about the research, the question then arose, how to get in touch with potential respondents? As a Black person, the writer knew many members of the Black community throughout the U.K., but felt that to use his acquaintance at this initial stage was not in keeping with the research endeavour. But the luck that all researchers need was present.

On the morning of November 1st 1980, while looking through the Prestwich Guide, (a local newspaper) the writer noticed an anniversary photograph of Mr. and Mrs. Bangbala with a brief history of Mr. Bangbala's life in Britain. This led to contact in which Mr. Bangbala agreed to participate in this research project. He also introduced the writer to Mr. Marke; Mr. Marke told the writer of Mrs. Locke, who informed of Mr. Faro's presence, and so on. So began the fieldwork; the researcher was now in the 'web'. While serendipity played a part, it was the research respondents that led to other respondents, 'I know of someone who could tell you much more about such things' was always a lead to meeting the next respondent. The writer had only one refusal. This was from a female member of one of the families in the study. She felt that projects such as this reveal too much of the community to the public gaze.

A problem was when to stop gathering information. Once in the 'web', members of the community were only too willing to talk. While this was gratifying, it was impossible to include all who were interested. The study was subject to constraints of time.

Heartful thanks are due to the respondents who gave so much of their time, and of themselves, in those interviews.

EDITOR'S NOTE : RALPH RUDDOCK

Don Henry's network method of contacting his subjects excluded any attempt at representivity. It resulted perhaps in some degree of homogeneity. It would appear that he was brought into contact with more of those who had succeeded in hammering their way through the system, with positive outcomes in great variety. The reader will soon come upon examples of failure however, most of which seem to be the outcome of deficiencies in the school system, and in teacher attitudes, rather than in the individual learner.

FURTHER READING BY DUNCAN SCOTT

Books and articles on the experiences of people of African and Caribbean descent in Britain reflect a number of influences. Chief among these are the origins of the authors - whether White British or African-Caribbean - and the varying significance attached by many of the latter to their homeland or roots. Cutting across these influences are ones of ideology and orientation.

Some writers emphasise their professional, literary and academic commitment, whilst others prefer to associate themselves more with combinations of national and community politics. For Black people in contemporary Britain, the concept of community is not simply a local and geographical matter; the common experiences of racism can have a unifying influence.

Don Henry's origins in the Caribbean did not restrict his investigations to those of Caribbean birth; indeed, more than half of the people whose voice we hear in this book were born in Britain. Five were born in Africa. Don's life experiences also enabled him to creatively bridge the academic-community divide. His roots in the Black community of Manchester, his struggle through the British education system, and his constant search for high literary standards, combine to provide a unique commentary on Black experiences in a White society.

The experience of people of African descent has been of interest to White historians of Britain for years, with Kenneth Little's **Negroes in Britain** (1947), James Walvin's various studies (1973-1984), and Peter Fryer's encyclopaedic **Staying Power** (1984) which also includes Asians.

Black writers have not ignored the subject, with Edward Scobie's **Black Britannia** (1972) and Folarin Shyllon's **Black Slaves in Britain** (1974) well worth seeking out. The debate on community or politically inspired writers on Black history was fuelled by Shyllon, who complained that White writers had ignored an earlier, Black, scholar, and had repeated liberal myths as history. Shyllon showed that slavery in England continued long after its alleged ending in 1772, a point that Eric Williams (later prime minister of Trinidad) had made in 1944. That Williams had his work widely available from 1964, that it was ignored by Richard West **Back to Africa** (1970), Roy Lewis and Yvonne Foy **The British in Africa**, (1971), and Frank Field and Patricia Haikin **Black Britons,** (1971), and that a bicentenary celebration of the so-called prohibition of slavery in Britain was organized by the Corporation of London in 1972, demonstrates how White historians have neglected both the truth and the work of Black writers.

Sadly, this same point has been made much more recently, in a critical commentary about the otherwise magnificent and ·newly-restored Liverpool Maritime Museum. As part of a report into race relations in the city of Liverpool Lord Gifford, Wally Brown and Ruth Bunday's **Loosen the Shackles** (1989) noted that the only souvenir postcard with a black face resembled a 1930's travel poster of a straw-hatted banana-boat man. References to the slave trade, in Liverpool's maritime past, were limited to the point of evasiveness.

Since the early seventies the debate on the merits or relative merits of Black and White commentators has continued. There is no White monopoly of historians now, with Scobie (born in Dominica, long resident in Britain), Shyllon from Nigeria, and the two tireless historians of Marcus Garvey and his movement from the 1920's, Tony Martin (born in Trinidad) and Robert Hill (born in Jamaica). The work of James Hooker, born in Trinidad, who wrote on the London residents Henry Sylvester Williams and

George Padmore, largely from a political angle, is also useful for those interested in Black British history.

Similarities in the experiences of visible minorities in Britain makes Ron Ramdin's passionate and political detail in **The Making of the Black Working Class in Britain** (1987) worth comparising and contrasting with Fryer.

In the field of local, community studies, it is useful to compare and contrast the work of the earlier studies (usually by White academics) with the more recent Black writers. Among the former are Little (1947) whose book was largely a study of Cardiff in the 1930's, Banton's **The Coloured Quarter** (1955) which was a Doctorate on Stepney (East London) supervised by Little, and Patterson's **Dark Strangers** (1963), which centred on Brixton.

Ken Pryce's **Endless Pressure** (1979) was one of the first of the new generation of Black academic studies, and dealt with the Black community of Bristol. His work and that of Stephen Small **Police and People in London**, (1983) demonstrates the different research strategies and dilemmas experienced by Black workers. For example, Small details his own arrest by the police whilst on a protest march.

Individual biographies by Black people include Edward Braithwaite **To Sir, With Love,** (1959); Eric Williams **Inward Hunger,** (1969), which tells of his years at Oxford in the 1930's; Ernest Marke **Old Man Trouble,** (1975); Beryl Gilroy **(Black Teacher,** (1976);Charles Ward **No Hardship in Being Black,** (1983); E. Martin Noble **Jamaica Airman,** (1984); Leslie Thompson **Leslie Thompson: an Autobiography,** (1985); and Robert Wellesley Cole **An Innocent in Britain,** (1988). Forthcoming is the autobiography of Rudolph Dunbar.

Marke, Thompson and Cole spent half a century in Britain. So did Learie Constantine, cricketer, lawyer and politician but his **Colour Bar** (1954) is not restricted to Britain. Constantine's friend C.L.R. James, also from Trinidad, spent decades in Britain,but again his writings are not restricted to Britain,

Both writers will be well-known to lovers of cricket. James, who died in May 1989, will surely have a biography. Until then, his **Beyond a Boundary** (1963) is the nearest, partly autobiographical, thing to it.

The experience of Black people in Britain, albeit through the eyes of White writers, can be seen in William Berwick Sayers **Samuel Coleridge-Taylor, Musician** (1915)

David Vaughan **Negro Victory** (1950), and Herbert Marshall and Mildred Stock **Ira Aldridge: The Negro Tragedian** (1958). Coleridge-Taylor (1875-1912) was a composer active in concert music, born of an African father in London, and an inspiration to fellow-Blacks around the world. Vaughan wrote of Dr Harold Moody (1881-1947), a Jamaican medical practitioner who settled in London in the 1910s, whose League of Coloured Peoples was active from 1931. Ira Aldridge, whose daughter inspired Scobie's **Black Britannia,** had a career in acting in mid-nineteenth century Britain. He was born in New York. Jack Birtley **The Tragedy of Randolph Turpin** (1975) tells of the Anglo-Guyanese Warwickshire-born boxing champion.

Views on immigrants include Joyce Egginton **They Seek A Living** (1957) which is concerned with African Caribbeans, and Colin Holmes **John Bull's Island: Immigration and British Society 1871-1971** (1988). Holmes also co-edits the Frank Cass journal **Immigrants and Minorities,** founded in 1981, which has published pieces on Blacks in Britain.

An often overlooked book, by the American Thomas J. Cottle, but published in London, **Black Testimony: Voices of Britain's West Indians** (1978), was based on his years in England 1975-1977. The Black experience of British schools is mentioned. Cottle believed that White investigators into Britain's Black communities would find that work more difficult in the future. That debate is concluded, according to some. If the quality of the work of Don Henry is the standard, there can be no justification for further questions.

Other Black researchers are active. Cecile Wright (1987) being a fine example. Williams (1988) expands the field to include youth and community work, and as his work is centred in London, where over two-thirds of African-Caribbeans of Britain have their homes, it is of considerable value.

Finally, it is important to underline the importance of the writings of novelists, and of commentaries from artists and community groups. Don Henry valued these territories most of all, seeing them as important in themselves, and important because of the absence of a well-developed Black professional commentary literature. The novels of Joan Riley **The Unbelonging,** (1985); **Waiting in the Twilight,** (1987); **Romance,** (1988) explore the variety of the African Caribbean experience including the life of

Black teenagers. Craven **Triangular Winds,** (1986) also uses the experiences for Blacks in and out of school. This last piece of 'community education' provides an appropriate conclusion, written and produced by Black young men and women contemporaries of Don Henry in Manchester.

BIBLIOGRAPHY
DON HENRY AND DUNCAN SCOTT

Allport, Gordon   **The Nature of Prejudice;**London, Allen, 1958

Arora, Ranjit and Carlton Duncan (eds)
    Multicultural Education; Towards Good Practice, London, Routledge, 1986.

Bailey, D.   'Rethinking Black Representations; From Positive Images to Cultural Photographic Practices' **'Ten-Eight** (Hockley, Birmingham)31, Winter 1988

Baker, John Randal   **Race** London, Oxford University Press, 1974.

Banton, Michael   **The Coloured Quarter; Negro Immigrants in an English City** London, Cape. 1955

Banton, Michael   **The Policeman in the Community,** London Tavistock, 1964

Banton, Michael   **Police - Community Relations,** London, Collins, 1973

Banton, Michael and Jonathan Harwood
                    The Race Concept Newton Abbot, David
                    and Charles, 1975.

Banton, Michael   **Racial   and   Ethnic   Competition**
                    Cambridge University Press, 1983.

Banton, Michael   'Racial Classification in the Census'
                    Social   Studies   Review Vol.1,No. 1,
                    1985, pp 21-25

Barker, Martin   **The New Racism** London, Junction Books,
                    1981.

Barton,Len and Stephen Walker (eds)
                    Race,   Class   and   Education London,
                    Croom Helm 1983.

Boggs, Carl   **Gramsci's Marxism** London, Pluto Press,
                    1976.

Bowker, Gordon   **Education   of   Coloured   Immigrant
                    Children** London, Longmans, 1968.

Carmichael, Stokely **Black   Power: The   Politics   of
                    Liberation   in   America,   London,
                    Pelican, 1969.

Cashmore, Ernest   **Black   Sportsmen** London,   Routledge,
                    1982.

Cashmore, Ernest and Barry Troyna (eds).
                    Black Youth in Crisis London,Allen and
                    Unwin, 1982.

Chipenda, J.   **Racism in Theology, Theology Against
                    Racism** London,   World   Council   of
                    Churches, 1975.

Church of England   **Faith in the City: A Call for Action
                    by Church and Nation** London, Church
                    House Publishing, 1985.

Coard, Bernard   **How the West Indian Child is made
                    Educationally   Sub-Normal   in   the
                    British School System** London, New
                    Beacon, 1971

Commission for Racial Equality
Further Education in a Multi-Racial Society: A Policy Report London, C.R.E., 1985.

Cone, James H.   **Black Theology of Liberation** Philadelphia, Lippincott, 1970

Craft, Maurice   'The Participation of Ethnic Minority Pupils in Further and Higher Education' **Journal of the National Foundation for Educational Research** Vol.25, No. 1, 1983, pp 10-21.

Craven J. (ed)   **Triangular Minds: Black Youth on Identity** Manchester, Caribbean English Project, 1986.

Cronin, Abby   'Supplementary Schools: Their Role in Culture Maintenance, Identity and Underachievement' **New Community** Vol. 11, No. 3, Spring 1984, pp 256-267.

Cross, Malcolm   'Black Youth Unemployment and Urban Policy' in **Unemployment and Racial Conflict in the Inner-City** Warwick University, Research Unit on Ethnic Relations.16, 1982.

Curtis, Stanley J.   **Education in Britain Since 1900** London, Dakers, 1952.

Dabydeen, David   'Underachievement: It's a Myth' **West Indian World** 24 April 1985.

Dahrendorf, Ralf   **Class and Conflict in Industrial Society** London, Routledge, 1959.

Daniel, William   **Racial Discrimination in England** London, Penguin, 1968.

Davis, Angela   **Women, Race and Class** London, Women's Press, 1982.

Department of Education and Science
The Education of Immigrants London, HMSO, 1971

Department of Education and Science
The Continuing Needs of Immigrants, HMSO, 1972

Dex, Shirley
'Second Chances: Further Education for Ethnic Minorities and the Labour Market' in Denis Gleeson (ed) Youth Training and the Search for Work London, Routledge, 1983

Dummett, Ann
A Portrait of English Racism London, Penguin, 1973.

Edwards, Paul (ed)
Equiano's Travels London, Heinmann, 1967.

Egginton, Joyce
They Seek a Living London, Hutchinson, 1957

Eggleston, John
'Anti-Racist Strategies for Further and Higher Education' Journal of the National Association of Teachers in Further and Higher Education, London, 1983.

Fryer, Peter
Staying Power: The History of Black People in Britain London, Pluto, 1984

Gershuny, J. and Raymond Pahl
'Work Outside Employment' New Universities Quarterly Vol 34 No. 1, 1980, pp 120-135.

Gifford, Lord, Wally Brown and Ruth Bundey
Loosen the Shackles: First Report of the Liverpool 8 Inquiry into Race Relations in Liverpool, London, Karia Press, 1989.

Giles, Raymond   **The West Indian Experience in British Schools** London, Heinemann, 1977.

Gilroy, Beryl   **Black Teacher** London, Cassell, 1976.

Gilroy, Paul   'Stepping Out in Babylon - Race, Class and Autonomy,' in George Lucas (ed) **The Empire Strikes Back: Race and Racism in 70s Britain** London, Hutchinson, 1982

Greater London Council

    Policing London 7, April-May 1983.

Gurnah, Ahmed   'Gatekeepers and Caretakers: Swann, Scarman and the Social Policy of Containment' in Barry Troyna (ed) **Racial Inequality in Education** (see below)

Hall, Stuart   **Drifting Into a Law and Order Society** London, Cobden Trust, 1979.

Halsey, Albert Henry **Change in British Society** London, Oxford University Press, 1978; 2d ed 1981; 3d ed 1986.

Harris, C.   'Images of Blacks in Britain: 1930-60' in Sheila Allen and Marie Macey (eds) **Race and Social Policy** London, Economic and Social Research Council, 1988

Hoch, Paul   **Rip-Off the Big Game: The Exploitation of Sports by the Power Elite** Garden City N.Y., Doubleday, 1972

Hodge, J.L.   **Cultural Bases of Racism and Group Oppression** Berkeley California, Two Riders Press, 1975.

Honeyford, Ray   'Education and Race: An Alternative View' **The Salisbury Review,** Winter 1984, pp 30-32

Husbands, Christopher
Race in Britain: Continuity and Change London, Hutchinson, 1982

Jacobs, Brian   **Racism in Britain** Cambridge University Press, 1987

James, C.L.R.   'Whither Trinidad and Tobago? **Race Today** Vol. 11, No. 4, November-December 1979, pp 111-115.

James, C.L.R.   **Spheres of Existence** London, Allison and Busby, 1980

Jeffcoate, Robert   **Ethnic Minorities and Education** New York, Harper and Row, 1984.

Jones, V.   **We Are Our Own Educators: From Supplementary to Black Complementary School** London, Karia Press, 1986.

Katznelson, Ira   **Black Men, White Cities: Race, Politics and Migration in the United States 1900-30 and in Britain 1948-68** London, Oxford University Press, 1973.

Kitwood, Tom and Carol Borrill
'The Significance of Schooling for an Ethnic Minority' **Oxford Review of Education** Vol 6, No. 3,1980, pp 241-255.

Lester,Anthony and Geoffrey Bindman
Race and Law London, Penguin, 1972

Lewis, Arthur   **Labour in the West Indies** London, New Beacon Books, 1977.

Little, Alan, R. Willey and J. Gundara
Adult Education and the Black Communities Leicester, Advisory Council for Adult and Continuing Education, 1982.

Little, Kenneth   **Negroes in Britain: A Study of Racial Relations in English Society** London, Kegan Paul, 1947.

MacDonald, C.   'Lisson Green Music Workshop' **Schooling and Culture** 13, 1983.

Marke, Ernest   **Old Man Trouble** London, Weidenfeld and Nicholson, 1975.

Martin, M.D. and J. Brain
                        Child Care and Health London, Hulton Education, 1983

Miles, Robert   'Racism and Nationalism in Britain' in Christopher Husbands **Race in Britain** (see above)·

Miles, Robert   **Racism and Political Action in Britain** London, Routledge, 1979

Mitchell, Clyde   'Case and Situation Analysis' **The Sociological Review** Vol 31, No. 2, 1983, pp 187-211

Moore, Robert   **Racism and Black Resistance in Britain** London, Pluto, 1975

Morrish, Ivor   **The Background of Immigrant Children** London, Allen and Unwin, 1971

Murray-Brown, Jeremy **Kenyatta** London, Allen and Unwin, 1972

Nkrumah, Kwame   **Ghana: The Autobiography of Kwame Nkrumah** Edinburgh, Nelson, 1957

Nkrumah, Kwame   **I Speak of Freedom** London, 1961

Open College of South London
                        Afro-Caribbean Perspectives on Education for Adults in South London, 1986

Patterson, Sheila   **Dark Strangers: A Study of West Indians in London** London, Penguin,1965

Pearson, D.

Race, Class and Political Activism: A Study of West Indians in Britain Aldershot, Gower, 1981

Phizaklea, Annie

Migrant Women and Wage Labour; The Case of West Indian Women in Britain London, Routledge, 1982

Poliakov, Leon

Aryan Myth: A History of Racist and Nationalist Ideas in Europe London, Heinemann, 1974.

Pryce, Ken

Endless Pressure London, Penguin,1979

Ramdin, Ron

The Making of the Black Working Class in Britain Aldershot, Gower, 1987.

Rampton Committee

West Indian Children in our Schools: Interim Report London, HMSO,1981.

Reeves, Frank

'Footprints in the Sand' in Roland Meighan (ed) **Perspectives on Society** London, Nelson, 1979.

Rex, John

'Race, Conflict and Plural Society' in Sami Zubaida (ed) **Race and Racialism** London, Tavistock, 1970

Rex, John and Sally Tomlinson (eds)
Colonial Immigrants in a British City London, Routledge, 1983.

Richmond, Anthony H. (ed)
Readings in Race and Ethnic Relations Oxford, Pergamon, 1972

Rodney, Walter

How Europe Underdeveloped Africa London, Bogle L'Ouverture, 1972

Rose, Jerry

Ghetto and the Underclass London, Routledge, 1988

Ruddock, Ralph

Evaluation: A Consideration of Methods and Principles Manchester University Department of Education 1981

Runnymede Trust   **Britain's Black Population** London, Heinemann, 1980

Rushdie, Salman   **The Political Papers** London, GLC Publications, 1985

Scafe, Suzanne   **Teaching Black Literature** London, Virago, 1989

Scarman Report   **The Scarman Report: The Brixton Disorders 10-12 April 1981** London, Penguin, 1981

Scobie, Edward   **Black Britannia: A History of Blacks in Britain** Chicago, Johnson Publishing 1972

Segal, Ronald Michael
     Race War London, Cape, 1966

Select Committee on Race Relations and Immigration
     Education London, HMSO, 1973

Shaw, John Peter G. Nordlie and Richard M. Shapiro (eds)
     Strategies for Improving Race Relations Manchester University Press, 1987.

Sheridan, P.   'Have and Have Nots:Careers Provision in a Midlands City' in Barry Troyna (ed) **Racism, School and the Labour Market** London, National Youth Bureau, 1983

Sherwood, Marika   **Many Struggles: West Indian Workers and Service Personnel in Britain 1939-1945** London, Karia Press, 1984

Shyllon, Folarin   **Black People in Britain, 1555-1833** London, Oxford University Press, 1977

Sivanandan, Ambalavaner
     A Different Hunger: Writings on Black Resistance London, Pluto, 1982

Sivanandan, Ambalavaner
'The Struggle for Black Arts in Britain' **Race and Class** Vol 30, 1986, pp 76-79

Small, Stephen **Police and People in London Vol 2: A Group of Young Black People** Policy Studies Institute, London, 1983

Solomos, John 'Institutionalised Racism: Policies of Marginalisation in Education and Training' in P. Cohen and H. Singh (eds) **Multi-Racist Britain** London, Macmillan, 1988

Stone, Maureen **The Education of the Black Child in Britain** London, Fontana, 1981

Stone, Maureen 'The Education of the Black Child in Britain ' in Alan James (eds) **The School in the Multi-Cultural Society** New York, Harper and Row, 1981.

Swann Report **Education for All** London,HMSO, 1985

Syer, Michael 'Racism, Ways of Thinking and School' in John Tierney (ed) **Race, Migration and Schooling** London, Holt, 1982

Taylor, Francine **Race, School and Community: A Study of Research and Literature,** Windsor, NFER Publishing, 1974.

Thomas, William I. and Florian Znaniecki **The Polish Peasant in Europe and America** Illinois University Press,1984

Thompson, Daniel C **Sociology of the Black Experience** Westport Ct. Greenwood Press, 1974

Tomlinson, Sally **Educational Subnormality: A Study in Decision Making** London, Routledge 1981

Tomlinson, Sally 'Race, Class and Education in Britain: A Bibliography' in Barton and Walker (eds) **Race, Class and Education** (see above.)

Troyna, Barry — 'Differential Commitment to Ethnic Identity by Black Youths in Britain' **New Community'** Vol. 3, No. 3, 1979 pp 424-428

Troyna, Barry — 'Fact or Artefact: The Educational Underachievement of Black Pupils' **British Journal of the Sociology of Education** Vol. 5, No. 2, 1984,pp 153-166

Troyna, Barry (ed) — **Racial Inequality in Education** London, Tavistock, 1987

Walvin, James — **Black and White: The Negro and English Society, 1555-1945** London, Penguin, 1973

Walvin, James — **Passage to Britain: Immigration in British History and Politics** London, Penguin, 1984

Ward, Charles — **No Hardship in Being Black,** London, Credo Consultants and Facto Books, 1983

Williams, Eric — **Capitalism and Slavery** London, Andre Deutsch, 1964

Williams, Lincoln — **Partial Surrender: Race and Resistance in the Youth Service** Lewes, Falmer Press, 1988

Wilson, Amrit — **Finding a Voice: Asian Women in Britain** London, Virago, 1978

Wilson, Amrit — 'In Between: The Mother in the Inter-Racial Family' **New Community** Vol. 9, No. 2, 1981, pp 36-43

Wright, Cecile — 'Black Students - White Teachers' in Barry Troyna (ed) **Racial Inequality in Education** (see above)

INDEX